CROSSCURRENTS *Modern Critiques*

CROSSCURRENTS *Modern Critiques*
Harry T. Moore, *General Editor*

Frederick J. Hoffman

Samuel Beckett
THE LANGUAGE OF SELF

WITH A PREFACE BY

Harry T. Moore

Carbondale and Edwardsville

SOUTHERN ILLINOIS UNIVERSITY PRESS

FEFFER & SIMONS, INC.

London and Amsterdam

To My Colleagues

in Literature and Philosophy,

UNIVERSITY OF CALIFORNIA,

RIVERSIDE

FIRST PUBLISHED, FEBRUARY 1962
SECOND PRINTING, JANUARY 1967

SAMUEL BECKETT'S career represents something rare enough to be almost incredible: He is an obscurantist whose plays fill theaters and whose novels sell widely. But perhaps he isn't really an obscurantist after all; perhaps we may attribute part of his success to his discovery and projection of the obscurantist elements in our life.

The very circumstances of Beckett's own life—since World War II, in which he was decorated for outstanding noncombatant service, he has lived in Paris virtually as a recluse—emphasize the elements of isolation and mystery found in his work. And it is perhaps significant that he is an Irishman who now writes almost entirely in French.

Technically, this friend of Joyce derives from the experimentalism of the 1920's. But, as Frederick J. Hoffman shows in this book, Beckett's subject matter has roots that go deeper into time. If Kafka's people are the cousins of Beckett's characters, their fathers and grandfathers are out of Dostoevsky.

Professor Hoffman has written several excellent books, including Freudianism and the Literary Mind (revised edition, 1957) and The Twenties (1955), but it seems to me that he has outdone himself in this fine study of Samuel Beckett, which both explicates Beck-

85196

ett's work and, as we have seen, relates it to important strains in the literature of our time and of the age just preceding.

As Mr. Hoffman observes, "the philosophical ground of twentieth-century literature has shifted from metaphysics to epistemology. Characters who were formerly maneuvered within an accepted frame of extraliterary reference are now represented as seeking their own language"—this is one of the keys to the understanding of Beckett, and one of the reasons why in spite of some of the surface difficulties we enjoy his writings. As Claude Mauriac has said, "It seems that with Samuel Beckett, whether we like it or not, even more than with Kafka or Joyce, we must exert ourselves." Note that: we must exert ourselves. Beckett, it may be observed, does not, like Kafka, deal in the allegory of a special sensitivity, nor does he, like the later Joyce, depend largely on curlicues of language. Rather, as Mauriac notes, Beckett's heroes, "interchangeable from book to book, are all projections of the author, who, in turn, is a reflection of ourselves." We are all waiting for Godot.

And indeed it is ourselves who are the real center of Frederick J. Hoffman's study, which examines Beckett's writing as one of the salient explanations of our existence, as far as it can be "explained." Professor Hoffman shows that Beckett has at least provided a new rhetoric for such explanations, with its own type of circumferential metaphors. The investigation of these matters, in both human and literary terms, is the contribution of the present book, an unusually penetrating and valuable study of one of our impressive contemporary masters and of the thought currents of his time.

HARRY T. MOORE

Southern Illinois University
May 24, 1961

CONTENTS

ACKNOWLEDGMENTS

BECAUSE of the kindness and efficiency of the library at the University of California, Riverside, I was able to get copies of Beckett's early works in good time; I am grateful to the librarians for their help. I am also indebted to the University for clerical assistance in the preparation of the manuscript.

As always, I am pleased to acknowledge the assistance of my good friend, Professor Warren I. Susman of Rutgers' department of history, whose intelligence about Beckett's meaning is not unexpectedly equal to his wisdom in other matters. On December 15, 1960, I was permitted to read sections of this book in a meeting of the Humanities Faculties Seminar at Riverside. The discussion which followed was very rewarding, and I want especially to thank Professors Philip Wheelwright, Herbert Lindenberger, David Harrah, Ben Stoltzfuss, and Egon Bittner for their contributions to it. In my dedication, I express a general debt of gratitude to the men who have made the beginnings of a new academic experience so rewarding and promising.

Mrs. Haverly Parker should especially be thanked for an expert and careful translation of my crabbed handwriting into eminently legible and neat typescript. I am as ever deeply grateful to my wife, for many expressions of love and patient care that have permitted me to survive the writing of this book, as they have made all of the others possible.

F. J. H.

SAMUEL BECKETT: *The Language of Self* is as much a book about its subtitle as its main title. In fact, the attention to them is almost equally divided. While I do not want to give the impression that Beckett merely serves as a text, his work is so strikingly an example of the *"fin de partie"* introspection so characteristic of recent literature that a study of him must take it rather elaborately into account.

The idea of this book grew out of an extended study, begun in 1957 and still in process, of the variants of death imagery and symbolism in modern literature. The third division of that book is called simply *Self*, but it involves elaborate speculations upon the fate of introspection in recent literature. Beckett's novels and plays seemed continuously to occur as the best, the most representative, illustrations of one aspect of that history. I became interested in him not merely because he has recently acquired a reputation, chiefly among theatre-goers—though surely the popular success of *Waiting for Godot* is a meaningful detail in recent intellectual history. His chief fascination lies in his having exhaustively explored a special variant of the drama of the self.

I have tried to define, in Chapters 1 and 2, the two major metaphors of twentieth-century self-analysis. The first of these is radically assertive of the powerful doubts hindering self-esteem in nineteenth-century literature. My discussion of it follows a line of descent from Dostoevsky's *Notes from the Underground* through late nineteenth-century examples to Kafka. There are special characteristics: The kinds of self-assertion and self-analysis expressed within it are highly emotional, melodramatic in a special sense. They argue a metaphysical despair which is stimulated by profoundly personal doubts of certain theological assurances. The point of almost all of the examples I have given in Chapter 1 is that the hero is personally engaged in a highly charged battle against both the rational "disease of consciousness" and the romantic doubts of divinity. I should call this type of self-analysis metaphysical and moral; this is true despite the elaborate semiepistemological discourse at the beginning of *Notes from the Underground*. The literary frame of these assertions is still recognizably traditional, though the drama contained within it may not be.

While this line of development is in large part dramatic, moral, and in a special sense "humanistic," the other major type of literary self-analysis is not. Or, it is not any of these things in any conventional literary sense. Instead, it is disputatious, inquisitive, and discursive. It is, in short, a kind of disquisition upon present residual elements of rationalism. I suppose a primary difference may be seen in the views taken in each case of the several metaphors of Christ, the Incarnation, the anthropomorphic prospects outlined in Christian theology. As I have tried to show in Chapter 1, a major crisis occurs when the divinity of Christ is seriously and emotionally questioned. If Christ after all shares our humanity, and if we cannot hope to profit from His divinity, then we are thrown into a desperate confusion of theological claims and counter-claims.

This is the line generally taken from Dostoevsky to Kafka and beyond, touching of course upon Beckett as well. But, in the case of a rationalist discourse that presupposes a once tightly constructed schematic system of physical and theological laws, the anthropomorphic exercise is limited, if it hasn't been quite definitely excluded. The principal line of inquiry of which Beckett's work is a significant consequence begins with Descartes; it comprises both the adventures of rational proof and the language of a disillusioned (or a largely inoperative) rational assertion. In several ways, the language of this kind of discourse is dissociated from its philosophical object. More important, rationalism detached from metaphysics diminishes to an epistemological inquiry. In its state of dislocation, the language ranges from a rather neatly coherent skepticism, to a frenzy of empty assertion, inquiry, and doubt: a babble, a stuck-needle or broken-weather-vane rhetoric. As the "I" is enlarged in literary strategies, confidence diminishes in its status of definition, and the language of inquiry is disengaged from traditional metaphysical systems of reference.

These observations (on which I attempt to elaborate in Chapters 2 and 3) are centrally relevant to Beckett's work. The novels (examined in Chapter 4) offer variations of what I have called the "residual Cartesian man"; there is a very clear development in them from recognizable narrative line to a torrent of verbalization. In the latter case, the novel is based on no definition, but only on doubt. Beckett's style retains the appearance of rational discourse throughout. There is a kind of frantic precision in all of them; but the "I's" of the trilogy are pathetically concerned with the apparent lack of true objectives in their inquiry.

The plays (discussed in Chapter 5) are a very different thing. Considering Beckett's work as a whole, one may describe a line leading from the extreme of words-without-acts to that of acts-without-words. The situations of both extremes are alike; the styles of representation radically differ. In either case, the purpose is much the same. And in the most recent work, we have such significantly descriptive titles as *Actes sans paroles* and *Textes pour rien*.

It is idle to ask what Beckett's novels and plays are "about." In any traditional or conventional sense, they are "about nothing"; they do not possess "human reference," as that phrase is customarily used. They presuppose no "society"; they are, for the most part, neither defenses of nor attacks upon society, civilization, culture, or class. Brendan Behan once said that if a man wanted entertainment, he might do worse than to see one of his plays; but if he wanted "lectures," he should visit Beckett's theatre.

This question has been quite honestly—and on at least one occasion in recent memory, intelligently—raised: what is the *worth* of this kind of exercise, if the novels and plays are "about nothing." My answer is that it is the most significant "nothing" in twentieth-century literature. Beckett's works are not empty intellectual exercises, but profound explorations of human intellectual dislocation. They are "about" a philosophical rhetoric set loose from its moorings; they are furthermore concerned with the dignified pathos of marginal man desperately trying to maintain his dignity and to find cause for it.

They are also "about" death—more accurately, annihilation. At the edge of death, the Beckettian self has no visible or tenable means of spiritual or intellectual support. A sociologist, who has been studying the problems of aging in what is sometimes callously labeled the "group of senior citizens," once told me that he was profoundly moved by *Endgame* as a dramatization of the gradual decline of consciousness, the terrifying specter of life's closing out, diminishing to the vanishing point. However valid that remark may be as a reaction to Beckett's play, it is true that his work is an analysis of the prospect of annihilation. But it is much more than that; in one sense, it is the tragicomedy of human deprivation, not so much of the *loss* of consciousness as of the *absence* of it. Beckett's heroes start with this "nothing," the "nothing new" mentioned in the first sentence of *Murphy*. The great new and distinctive contribution he makes to modern literature lies in the *style* of his novels and plays: both are essentially concerned to produce the impression of the residual self, the final expressions of a rudderless and purposeless intellect. The novels give the rhetoric of this situation, the plays, its varied gestures. Despite the implications of Behan's remark, Beckett is a master of comedy. The "metaphors of the circumference" are very different from Emerson's "metaphors of the center," but they are as truly appropriate to Beckett's literary situation as Emerson's were to his.

I have tried to communicate these impressions in the book that follows. It is altogether possible that Beckett has initiated a new form of literary discourse, calling upon new resources for its comprehension. In this sense, he is an innovator, who has offered constitutive literary situations and manners that need to be accepted on their own terms, not on traditional grounds. If my study has done no more than "locate" Beckett within the modern history of the self's language, I shall be more than pleased.

Frederick J. Hoffman

The University of California,
Riverside
December 23, 1960

Samuel Beckett
THE LANGUAGE OF SELF

THE UNDERGROUND MAN:
BACKGROUND OF THE
MODERN SELF

THERE ARE MANY possible beginnings. Any one of a
number of incidents in the literature of the last century might serve to dramatize the special and very
complex issues and languages of the modern self.
Nineteenth-century Russian literature offers a usefully
consistent and varied succession of events, none so
pertinent as Dostoevsky's *Notes from the Underground* (1864).[1] Especially relevant is the narrator's
accidental meeting with a young prostitute.

Consider the circumstances of the affair. The narrator has arrived after a feverish pursuit of men whom
he wishes to insult so that he may assert his own identity and importance. They have gone, and instead he
is left with Lisa, a twenty-year-old girl from Riga, "a
fresh, young, somewhat pale face, with straight dark
eyebrows, and with a serious, as it were, surprised look
in her eyes." As he walks up to her, he sees himself
momentarily in a mirror: "My flustered face looked
utterly revolting to me: pale, evil, mean, with di-
shevelled hair. 'It's all right, I'm glad of it,' I thought.
'I'm glad that I'll seem repulsive to her.'"

He begins to "lecture" her, delivers a sermon on the
hazards of prostitution, its role in destroying love. A
tortured and contradictory man, he has become for the
moment a righteous savior of his fellow creatures. All

of this is an assertion of self, a momentary expression of a superiority; it is above all an affectation of sincerity strategically indulged by the narrator in the interests of defining identity. Sentimental and cynical by turns, he is, as it were, watching himself in the mirror of his mind; he carefully stages both the tone and the effect of his delivery. At the same time he shivers "as though in a fever and almost in terror" at the thought that Lisa may be taking him seriously, in other words that his performance may be proved a success.

The underground man is a contradictory man. Nothing may satisfactorily be said of him because, as he says, he suffers from the "disease" of consciousness which acts from the start against his being clearly one person or another. Almost all of his energy is devoted to the effect he as a self achieves in terms of himself as observer. He is defeated by the mirror of self-will. There is no place for him, no area of human activity in which his talents, his peculiarities of self, may be of service. The brothel scene and the room in which the underground man lives are interchangeable: dingy, dark, cluttered with objects of indifferent value, these rooms enclose and inhibit life; they are a means of withdrawal from life, but they are also a life-surrogate. They become, in the history of the modern hero, the world itself, the scenic image of a reduced and contracted self.

The strange meeting of the two deprived selves is repeated when Lisa—impressed by his eloquence, more than half convinced of his sincerity—visits him in his lodgings, the "unfurnished self-contained flat" as he calls it, "my shell, the case in which I hid from humanity." Again the encounter is not anticipated; she appears unexpectedly, when he is in the midst of a stupid and exhausting quarrel with his servant. Here, in his own setting, she sees him: "I stood before her,

feeling utterly crushed, disgraced, and shockingly embarrassed, trying desperately to wrap myself in the
skirts of my tattered, wadded old dressing gown,
exactly as a short while ago in one of the moments of
complete depression I had imagined I would do."

His disreputable state of dress, or undress, is of the
utmost importance to him, as it is to our image of
him. He has always put great stress upon what he
might call "adequate clothing"; in his most pathetic
moments he is discovered in shabby dress, his entire
personality "en déshabillé." To him clothes are a
matter of advantage or disadvantage; they signify
degrees of status. Lisa has discovered him in a state of
deprivation, as though he had suffered a disastrous
change, from man to insect, not very different from
the impression Kafka's Gregor Samsa makes upon his
family on the fateful morning of his metamorphosis.

One may appreciate in this experience a constant
interplay of fragmented selves. The underground man
is aware of himself as a "louse" or a "fly," a mean
creature; but his awareness is always countered in one
way or another by a form of assertion. He rescues
amour-propre by an access to the worst display of sentimentality. Having been caught at a disadvantage, he
converts it into a display of self-pity. He sobs over the
obvious evidences of his poverty and mean status. At
the same time, as in the first encounter, he is play-
acting and shifting the blame of his embarrassment
upon her. If he must be caught in a state of misery, he
will have to exploit it fully; the worm turns, upon the
virtue of its wormhood:

> Nor shall I ever forgive *you* for what I'm now confess-
> ing to you! Yes, you alone must answer for it all because
> you just happened to come at that moment, because I'm
> a rotter, because I'm the most horrible, the most ridicu-
> lous, the most petty, the most stupid, the most envious

of all the worms on earth who are not a bit better than
me, but who—I'm damned if I know why—are never
ashamed or embarrassed, while I shall be insulted all
my life by every louse because that's the sort of fellow
I am!

This extraordinary display can best be described as
expedient self-abasement. There is as much truth in it,
and as little, as there had been in his brothel sermon.
He is in the act of asserting a superior inferiority, one
of the many paradoxes by means of which he nour-
ishes his identity. Dostoevsky wants, here and
throughout, to describe a condition of extreme self-
willing, a flagrant violation (and at the same time an
exploitation) of reason and propriety, and above all
an honest portrait of the ambiguities of self-rational-
ization. He is neither sympathetic nor hostile to the
underground man. The anti-hero is what he is for
many reasons, not the least of which is the circumstance of his setting—the urban world of furnished
and unfurnished rooms, of dark and dingy holes,
caves, and cellars in which so many souls hide from an
external world to which they cannot or will not aspire.
The point is that the underground man *wills*; however
distorted and ingeniously tortured (and comical) his
postures and gestures are, they are willed; they are not
rational or logical or predictable.

In his painstaking attention to this dingy psychological décor, Dostoevsky has a double purpose, to
defy the confident prophets of a reasonable world and
to portray the disasters of an uninstructed and distorted self-will. The sad appearance of the willing self
in these circumstances is a paradigm of the modern
consciousness. It is above all important to note that
the distresses of self-consciousness, as these are so
abundantly given in his fiction, are largely a consequence of an altogether inadequate, even a petty and

mean, circumstance. The self wills its peculiarity, but that peculiarity is only as distinguished as circumstances permit it to be. Dostoevsky would have us believe that distortions of the will occur from one of two major causes: either from a hideously inflated sense of the power of the intellect or from a petty confusion of cross-purposes and in-purposes which consume the self in exercises of pitiful and inept assertion. Both causes relate to a prior and primary one, the all but total loss of belief in and respect for a transcendent being who might be relied on to alleviate the tortures of felt and sensed mortality.

ii

The underground man is peculiarly the victim of a persistent and hopeless awareness of mortality. The power of the will, the testimony to which is the most important vision of *Notes from the Underground*, is in his case turned almost entirely inward. He has been given the present of a will, indeed devotes much of his energy to an assertion of it. He will not and cannot subscribe either to rational schemes which advocate a brilliant new social future or to the disciplines of stoic moral containment. He is romantically inclined to rebellion, which is in his case a distortion of the will to isolated selfhood, but he is at the same time held by the realistic circumstances of his age and kind. In a curious and even a distorted way, the underground man renounces both the real world (of which he is nevertheless a victim) and the prospects of a world as it "reasonably should be," in favor of what amounts to a perverse interest in tortured self-analysis.

The two major symbols of this condition are wall and mirror. The glass and steel structure of London's Crystal Palace is a symbol of all that the underground man hates. It is a product of rational human effort and a portent of an even more formidably impressive future. More than that, it objectively testifies to the power of the *contained* will—which is to say, in the vocabulary of the underground man, the thwarted and suppressed will. It is exclusively and forbiddingly a structure of the "will to good." The Crystal Palace is an extreme example of the rational wall. Specifically, in the setting of Petersburg or Moscow, the wall is imaged as the room—itself walled in in a thousand ways—in which the underground man lives. Again and again, the Dostoevskian scene testifies to the strength of such enclosures. The anti-hero knocks his head against this wall, or he gives testimony of his surviving self in the disorder of the room surrounded by walls. He *suffers* the wall, and in suffering testifies to himself as a sentient being. The wall is therefore a testimony of the rational equation. Two plus two equal four. He does not accept the equation, but he suffers it. As the wall rationally encloses space, so it shuts off light and air and encourages the belief in a condition of an absolute impurity of self. The room is a cave, a cellar, and in implication a womb. As womb, however, it suggests a perversion of biological and maternal function. It protects the self in the absolute sense of preventing self-realization. To remain within such a space is to prevent self-completion. The self remains isolated, and the "others" to whom it should normally have access for its development become irritants and perverse challenges to self-will. By means of a dream or fantasy transition, the wall becomes a mirror. The underground man becomes a romantic hero (a "King of Spain," in Gogol's sketch, "The Diary of a Madman") in his dreams, which are nourished by his search for complementary texts. These dreams are a surrogate world which enables him to transcend the circumstances of his room without leaving it. When the external world—of bureaucratic manners, social protocol, or family affairs—threatens to intrude, the underground man is ready to meet it self-defensively. Lisa is a mirror in which the underground man sees only the effects of a closed self.

The wall shuts him off from a world in which he does not find it possible or convenient to believe; within the walled enclosure, the mind collaborates with a mirror surface to enact again and again the tragicomedy of the underground self. In Dostoevsky's case, this self is both pathetically vulgar and preciously heroic. There is no better example in literature of an author's ambivalent attitude toward his hero. He is both despicable and comically admirable in his gestures of self-sustenance. In his acts of willing he asserts a defiant selfness against the mediocrity of his surroundings; but in willing his status as self he essentially wills only that he exist *as* self. He neither accepts responsibility for being a self nor extends his selfness within the world of "others."

He wishes, above all, to assert himself as at the center of his universe. In its expressions in Dostoevsky and other nineteenth-century Russian literature, this figure is a superb example of the struggle of the self against marginality. In any genuine and ultimate sense, the fight of the self against the threat of his being pushed off center and toward the margin of reality is, once again, a variant upon man's basic fear of mortality. In the elaborate Swedenborgian exercises of the elder Henry James, the self *is* divine in the sense that God actualizes himself in it. Whatever the variations upon this theme, in Emerson, Thoreau, Whitman, one is left with the impression of an expanding, projecting ego, who creates in the act of *seeing* creation—that is, who both sees and makes the forms of the world which he comprehends. For the most part, contemporary Russian views of the self begin from another, a quite decisively different, vantage point. It has been settled upon, to begin with, that the self is constrained by a physical, mortal body which is hopelessly unable to transcend the move toward corruption. The body is on the way to becoming a "stinking corpse"; as matter dissolves, the mind and spirit loses value and function.

These are not unique circumstances. In all literature of the nineteenth century, the self is shown reacting in either of two ways to the threat of marginality: romantic despair over the prospect of death, or an introspective fastidiousness over comprehension of self in the most melancholy of natural circumstances. The selves of Pushkin and of Lermontov give in to Byronic introspection and act impulsively within vast spaces and on a large scale of heroic opportunity. They are self-willed, but their acts are in a way a romantic vindication. In any absolute sense, these heroes are "superfluous men," but the romantic pose demands that it is the world and not they who are superfluous.

Two changes occur in the development of the nineteenth-century representation of self. On the one hand, the romantic hero becomes the "superfluous man"; that is, the very nature of his romantic despair, disillusion, or melancholy is shown to come from an "unproductive" or an "unrealistic," in any case an "unprofitable" set of circumstances. He does no one any good and the scope of his emotional extravagances is judged as tedious and perhaps a bit ridiculous. Turgenev's Bazarov (*Fathers and Sons*) rather definitively "sets down" the residue of romantic manners as they persist in Kirsanov's "code."

More significant is the figure of the underground man, whose rebellion against encroachments upon self-esteem is of a quite different character. The setting is radically changed, for one thing; it becomes urban, spatially reduced and congested. Almost by necessity, space and light yield to wall and darkness. Further, the "code" of the romantic is replaced by the petty manners and intrigues of bureaucracy. These souls, deprived of both space and scope in their maneuvers, act feverishly and with fastidious decorum in a world of petty privilege and rank. They become superfluous to the world as well as to themselves. In one of their many variants, they are, like Gogol's Akakii Akakiievich ("The Overcoat" [2]), so inconspicuously humdrum that they lose identity altogether in the anonymity of their function: "No matter how many Directors and his superiors of one sort or another came and went, he was always to be seen in the one and the same spot, in the same posture, in the very same post, always the Clerk of Correspondence, so that subsequently people became convinced that he evidently had come into the world just the way he was, all done and set, in a uniform frock and bald at the temples."

This drab and anonymous being, of interest to no one, not even to "a naturalist who wouldn't let a chance slip of sticking an ordinary housefly on a pin," does nevertheless have a brief experience of self-glory, but he serves primarily as a caution to the entire structure of bureaucratic mores and manners. The threat of anonymity is the principal cause of undergroundling discontent. Failing the proper kind of rescue through inheritance or other good fortune, the bureaucrat has recourse to fantasy and dream, in which he imagines himself either as a superior being or as a master-victim of the chicanery of his fellows.

Gogol's "A Madman's Diary" combines the two modes of rebellion: "A queer notion you have got into your head that no one is a gentleman but yourself. Give me a fashionably cut coat and let me put on a cravat like yours—and then you wouldn't hold a candle to me. I haven't the means, that's the trouble." [3]

This form of rationalization leads eventually to a persecution mania, to which are added delusions of power. The madman of Gogol is Dostoevsky's undergroundling compounded. He becomes the "King of Spain" in his fantasies, and he conquers all men and women in the world of his spent vision. In the end, he suffers the tortures of the cure in an asylum, and these are the final agony of his role as victim. The attendant becomes his "Grand Inquisitor," and the pain of the cure is confused with his role as victim on the rack.

These fantasies lead to another important variant of the underground self—the double. Partly the *dédoublement* of underground sensibility is a consequence of the general anonymity suffered. Partly it is an extension of the mirror symbol. The bureaucrat sees himself *in* the role of his superior, he sees his inferior in *his* role. Most of all, he sees himself repeated endlessly in the corridors of an insufferable way of life, and his ambition—to be his superior—collides with his exhausting boredom. The double (as in Dostoevsky's early novel) is an aspect of the self, suppressed perhaps but not too skillfully, who interferes with the peace and the security of the self. The double is an ever-present reminder of the sins of self-omission, of the sacrifice of completeness for the sake of prudent self-interest.

Perhaps the most cutting irony in the Russian treatment of social negation occurs in Gogol's *Dead Souls* (1842). It is a kind of trickery that is itself caused by a basic cruelty, the habit of considering human beings as commodities, as "souls" in the sense of cattle. Dead souls are the names of dead serfs who officially remain on the tax rolls until the next tax census. Pavel Ivanovich Chichikov, himself a bureaucratic adventurer, like most others of Gogol's creatures conniving to escape anonymity, initiates a gigantic hoax. Surely it is a trick undertaken in full awareness of the basic irony of its object; for the men and women who sell him these dead souls are only infrequently misled by the deception. The dead souls may be called commodities bargained for by the Devil, of whom Chichikov is authorized representative. In any case, there is no moral awareness, no "spirit" involved either in the purchase or in the sale of dead souls. The entire world of Gogol's novel is dead, and in this sense the transactions may be described as legitimate.

iii

In this analysis of the marginal self, the famous hero of Goncharov's novel *Oblomov* (1859) [4] has a special value. He is the supreme case of the "superfluous man," the man at furthest remove from the world of active decision or a purposeful life. As Henry Gifford says of him (*The Hero of His Time*), "The activity of ordinary life repelled Oblomov. He had infinite dreams, and infinite excuses."

The struggle between purpose and inaction in this novel is crucial to the Russian analysis of the marginal self. The leftist analyses of Oblomovism stress a significant factor of the condition. N. A. Dobrolyubov, in his essay, "What Is Oblomovism?" (1859) intended an indictment of all superfluous heroes who acted from selfish motives; but his analysis of the relation of character to reality can serve well to define the problem of the marginal self. Dobrolyubov maintained that, in the light of the artist's responsibility to the "real world," he was always responsible to its fictional counterpart. Therefore, a character who acted selfishly in a novel sinned against the social responsibilities of the actual world. Novelists like Goncharov do well to point up these genuine defections, but they have done only a small part of the job. The next step is to answer the need for "positive heroes," who, by acting meaningfully in their fictional world, will stimulate purposeful action in the real.

The truly important distinction made by Dobrolyubov is between outer and inner reality. Quite aside from the kinds of definition available to each, the Russian analysis of the self is essentially in terms of the relationship between these two realities. It is more complex than Dobrolyubov and his contemporaries thought. Essentially it involves the manner in which the inner self makes its stamp, or impression, upon outer reality. This impression varies with degree of maturity in the self. It must also be true that there is some hypothetically ideal condition in the relationship in which the two realities achieve perfect equilibrium. But this balance is scarcely to be hoped for, and in any case the hope of one argues a perfectly adjusted, and therefore a quite "harmless," society. Degrees of imbalance are, however, abundantly in evidence in Russian literature. The scope of imbalance depends largely upon the scene itself of the tragicomedy. The outer reality presses upon the inner, and should stimulate a compensating outward pressure. But it is more than likely to extend the scope of inner reality itself— in short, to force a withdrawal of the self into a protective minimum semblance of outwardness.

In Oblomov's case, the inner reality is almost entirely protective. Action, purpose, efficiency, schedules, improvements, the "actualization of ideals"— these are all threats to the self. They upset it and

menace its desire for tranquil and easeful "fulfilment."
In the long stretches of Part One of Goncharov's
novel, Oblomov spends his time deciding whether he
shall arise at all for the day. A procession of figures
moves in and out of his lodgings, some of them urging
him to start his day, others asking that he attend to
one or another obligation. These importunities cause
him momentary anxiety—and he is so overcome by
distressful weariness that he must return to his sofa.
"If his mind was troubled, his eyes were clouded over,
lines appeared on his forehead, and he was plunged
into doubt, sadness, and fear; but his anxiety seldom
took the form of any definite idea and still more
seldom was it transformed into a decision. All his
anxiety resolved itself into a sigh and dissolved into
apathy or drowsiness." (*pp. 13–14*)

This tendency to resume the horizontal as the best
position from which to contemplate the world is of
course Oblomov's besetting sin; if the novel can be
said to have a theme, it is the struggle to rouse Oblomov to a full awareness of outer pressures. The struggle often has the quality of incidental comedy routines, such as this parody of Hamlet's plight: " 'Now
or never!' 'To be or not to be!'—Oblomov raised himself from his chair a little but failing to find his slip-
pers with his feet at once, sat down again." (*p. 187*)

Mostly, however, the conflict is between those who,
like the energetically good Stolz, wish to bring out the
"buried good" in him, and the trickster who wishes to
defraud him of his last penny. Oblomov is susceptible to either kind of pressure, and he goes a long way
in allowing Stolz to make a full-fledged man of him.
Through Stolz's good graces, Oblomov is forced from
his bed and into the open air, to engage in the most
strenuous and the most anxious of all of his essays into
outer reality. It involves a tortured and tortuous love

affair with Olga, which quite overrules his desire for rest and tranquillity. "He had not for many years felt so alive and strong—his strength seemed to be welling out from the depths of his soul ready for any heroic deed." (195–96)

But her love causes him more anxiety than joy. It is foreign to his nature, and against his will, to bestir himself constantly to pay court and put questions to a beloved. His response to Olga is a mixture of anxieties —that he should fail her ideal and that he should succeed with her and thus destroy his peace of mind forevermore. In a long and eloquent letter to her, which genuinely expresses his fears, Oblomov defines his anxious state of mind: "Love makes incredible progress, it is a kind of gangrene of the soul. Now I am in as bad a state as can be . . . All this is all right for youth, which bears easily pleasant and unpleasant sensations; what I want is peace and quiet, however dull and somnolent, for it is familiar to me; for I cannot weather storms." (248–49)

He is, in short, afraid of passion, as a disturbance of the soul; and he gratefully yields to the motherly Agafya, of the fat white elbows and the respectful, timid smile, who takes over from Olga, to nurse and nourish him to the end of his days. Agafya is the perfect realization of Oblomov's dream of Oblomovka, the place of his childhood. It is a country place, placid and quiet, where talk is not agitated, sleep frequent, and death occurs, if at all, "as if by stealth."

> At midday it was hot; not a cloud in the sky. The sun stood motionless overhead scorching the grass. There was not the faintest breeze in the motionless air. Neither tree nor water stirred; an imperturbable stillness fell over the village and the fields, as though everything were dead. (114)

Men of forty looked like boys; old men did not struggle
with a hard, painful death but, having lived to an un-
believably old age, died as if by stealth, quietly growing cold and imperceptibly breathing their last. (124)

This vision of tranquillity marks a static image of
withdrawal, into a kind of inactivity, or minimum activity, to which Oblomovism tends. The kindly and
energetically good Stolz strives vainly to separate
Oblomov from the vision; and in the end he has withdrawn entirely, into death. His career, drawn not un-
sympathetically by Goncharov, was the perfect target
for leftist contemporaries. Obviously this was to them
the most willful of superfluous men. Rufus Mathewson, drawing principally from Belinsky, has described
a composite figure of the revolutionary "good hero."
In every respect the antithesis of Oblomov, this man
manifests a kind of "cheerless optimism," expecting
that society will and must move "forward and up-
ward"; he is a man of "service," aware that history
must be prodded and abetted; he is above all a "representative man":

> He will not be a sovereign, a lawgiver, or a conqueror,
> but a man much closer to his fellows in ranks and abili-
> ties, distinguished from them only by the firmness of his
> convictions and the force of his character. He will not
> be the "brilliant exception," or the man touched by
> genius, or the man set apart by innate or supernatural
> qualities. He will be rather the "first among equals," a
> representative man.[5]

It is easy to see in this portrait the man who wills
the future, who goes beyond the self without the
thought of self-aggrandisement, who denies himself
the slightest temptation of superfluity. He is a singu-
larly bloodless and colorless creature, but he is the antithesis of all those men who haunt the crevices and

cellars of the "underground" or crowd against each other in the Nevsky Prospect. What inspired hostility to him in all great Russian artists, from Turgenev to Tolstoi, was his complete submission to the stereotype of necessity. The tendentiousness of criticism could go no further than this assertion, by Chernyshevsky: "The beautiful is that in which we see life as we understand it and wish it" (*Aesthetic*). The hero Rakhmetov of Chernyshevsky's novel, *What Is to Be Done?* (1863), is the paragon of flawless social purpose, a rare man but a necessary one. He subordinates the self to the will of the future, guided by rational principle. By long study of good sound books, he enters a state of selfless grace, according to which he moves beyond the trivialities and agonies of the self-willed marginal man, to serve the total society of the future: "Consciously and firmly he decided to renounce all the advantages and honors which he might have demanded of life in order to work for the benefit of others, finding his own greatest interest in the pleasure from that kind of work."

This creature of absolute principle is of course made entirely from outer reality, as Oblomov proves eventually to be fashioned altogether from inner. He is the model to be set against both Hamlet and Don Quixote, and he has of course entirely overcome the temptations of "Oblomovitis." While Rakhmetov is designed essentially as an ideal heroic figure for political activists, he is also created from the necessity to find an alternative to the varieties of marginal personality created by Gogol, Goncharov, Chekov, Dostoevsky, and Turgenev. Rakhmetov and the underground man of Dostoevsky stand in dialectical opposition in the struggle to define and discover the hero of their time. The inner necessity yields altogether to outward pressure in Chernyshevsky. In Goncharov's novel, irony plays lightly upon Oblomov's retreat before the disturbance of the effectual Stolz. Dostoevsky's anti-hero has, however, absorbed outer pressures to the end of his acting altogether from spiteful or assertive self-will. Each of these characters falls far short of a balance of inner and outer selves, but they are all, taken together, a remarkable composite vision of the vicissitudes assumed by the will in nineteenth-century Russian society.

iv

The truly superfluous man suffers from the defective consequences of his humanity. He is after all too "human" to assume the responsibilities of ideological virtue. Both Turgenev and Dostoevsky, in very different ways, described the tragedy of man's falling short of various kinds of ideological demand. The Dostoevskian hero is often a victim of his extraordinary sensitivity to human suffering, which causes him either to renounce an absolutist principle or to go mad. On a level above that of Gogol's bureaucrats, Turgenev's and Dostoevsky's heroes enact genuine and meaningful tragedies caused primarily by the failure of human perfectibility.

In both cases, the major concern of tragedy is the recognition of mortal limits—or, to see it in another way, the desperate struggle to strengthen belief in either a God or a transcendent principle. The famous quarrels of Turgenev and Dostoevsky are primarily concerned with their radical differences over the question of "Western" reason and sophistication. "For my part," Turgenev wrote to Pauline Viardot, "I prefer Prometheus, I prefer Satan to a capricious and autocratic Deity, the prototype of revolt and individuality. Atom though I am, I am my own master, I want truth and not salvation, and I expect to get it from my reason and not from grace." [6]

This of course is a position radically different from Dostoevsky's; it is, in fact, the *bête noir* of the underground man's rebellion. It is a Western and not a Russian concept of individuality. Turgenev could not always believe in it, but he did suggest more frequently than not the need for what he called "*consciously* heroic natures in order that things should move forward." [7] He was too sensitively aware of human limitations to go the whole way, toward the blameless and bloodless Chernyshevsky paragon.

The major block to human perfection, in Turgenev's mind, is death. Death plays a monstrous role in his fictions, whether to cut off a "consciously heroic" ambition (*On the Eve*), to cut down in an almost trivially accidental way a life of promise (*Fathers and Sons*), or, as in suicide, to provide the way out of an impossibly tangled situation (*Virgin Soil*). In the strange piece called *Enough* (mocked several times in Dostoevsky's work), he speaks with an almost adolescent despair of the fatality of human life, the impossibility of art's attempts to arrest nature and make formal sense of the world: "When all is said and done, nature is irresistible; there is no need for her to be in a hurry; sooner or later she will take what is hers; she creates while destroying, and it makes no difference to her what she creates or what she destroys so long as life does not perish, so long as death does not forfeit its rights."

Because he of all Russian contemporaries was "Western" in spirit, and because, despite his announced confidence in "the reason," he noted the human tendency to fall short of perfection, Turgenev is admirably suited to the task of exploring the genuine defects of the reasonable self, the hero of social change. In a real sense, Turgenev analyzed the processes according to which the rational self, unlike its Marxist prototype, shifted its position from center to margin. This is because almost all of his heroes fail to make their central convictions hold up, whether for themselves or for others.

Bazarov of *Fathers and Sons* (1862) [8] is a superb illustration of the man of rational arrogance who displaces the gentleman, only to be himself cancelled arbitrarily by death. There is so absolute an appropriateness in Bazarov's dying of an "accident" that the shift from center to margin of his precious ego is remarkably and clearly seen and explained in it. To begin with, Bazarov has taken over quite thoroughly the position of the "new man," who will become useful and meaningful by mastering materialistic procedures. He will stand no nonsense in the matter of codes or manners or beauty. "A good chemist is more useful than a score of poets," he says in one place (*p. 28*). Nature is not a temple, but a workshop. Even when he is quite overcome by the beauty of Mme. Odintzov, he remarks: "A really opulent body! . . . Just ripe for the dissecting table" (*92*).

It is admirably fitting that Bazarov should find his antagonist in one of Turgenev's "superfluous men," Pavel Petrovich Kirsanov. Kirsanov ideally represents several of the gestures of the decadent romantic, including Oblomov's of withdrawing from anxiety: "He threw himself down on a sofa, put his hands to his head and remained quite motionless, staring almost in despair at the ceiling. Whether he wished to conceal the expression on his face from the very wall or for some other reason, he got up, unfastened the heavy window-curtains, and then again slumped back on the sofa." (*46*) The contrast is more than one of generations; they are representatives of quite anti-thetic ways of life. And their antagonism is exquisitely and comically rendered in the duel scene, caused in itself by the elaborately archaic buffoonery of an anti-quated code of manners. The code is necessary to "satisfy Kirsanov's honor," but also to keep Bazarov from killing him outright. In the end, Bazarov has quickly to change roles, from man of honor to man of science, to attend Kirsanov's wound. The conscien-tious attention to protocol is a graceful overtone of this conflict of heroes.

We may reconstruct the duel scene in terms of the two selves, each combating for a central position in his world. In so maneuvering his code as to make a duel with Bazarov necessary, Kirsanov has made his last major self-assertion; at stake are his self-esteem and the elaborate formalities with which he protects it. Bazarov, uncomfortable in his role of formal an-tagonist, risks the position of his "new self" by assum-ing it; but he is shortly returned to his proper center when Kirsanov is wounded and he must attend him. So that Kirsanov, whose self-respect is insulted by Bazarov's presence, momentarily moves from margin to center, then—as seems fitting in a contest that would not have tolerated so gross an irony—returns to the position of "superfluous man."

Turgenev's maneuvering of selves does not stop here. There are momentary glances at unsavory revolu-tionary types, but the major irony is reserved for Bazarov's death. Here Turgenev's haunting sense of the arbitrary role of mortality over all human preten-sion is fully actualized. In his dying, caused by sloven-liness on the part of the village doctor, Bazarov is at once removed from his "center," to become what he has thought all men and women were: corruptible and moribund accumulations of physical substance: "How strange! I want to concentrate and think of death, but I can't even do that. I merely see a patch of sorts . . . and that's all." (233) When Madame Odintzov arrives, he can do no more than persist in the ironic position he has always held: "Well, what shall I say to you? . . . I was in love with you! That made little sense before, even less now. Love has a body, and my particular body is already disintegrating." (239) Bazarov dead has been conquered by the principles of Bazarov living. His place in the village graveyard is covered with weeds, his body and mind have long since departed. Only the attention of his aging parents testifies to the possibility of a transcendent power.

The major irony of Turgenevs' novel has to do with the displacement of Bazarov's personality, in accordance with the very principles he has arrogantly assumed in his lifetime. He has argued the materiality of matter and the futility of forms from the beginning. In the end his body testifies to the correctness of his assertions, but at the expense of his self-esteem. The only forms left are those adhered to by his parents, who stare humbly and uncomprehendingly at his grave. In many ways, Bazarov is a throwback to Pushkin's Onegin and Lermontov's Pechorin, romantic heroes but like him in the strength of self-concern and pride. Bazarov is also self-centered, but with an almost total absorption in his own convictions. His is not a transcendentalist but strictly a materialist vision; it leads nowhere, except perhaps incidentally to a kind of "public service," and its apparent function is to gratify an egocentric person, a rebel against all forms except those which circumscribe the world of experimental science.

Turgenev assumes that human ambition and pretension, whatever their moral color, are curtailed by mortality; and in each of his major novels the hero's status is qualified, though his stature may not be affected, by evidences of his role as mortal being. The great effectiveness of *On the Eve* (1859) comes from this fact, as it relates to Insarov (who dies before he can be of much use), but mostly for its effect on the heroine, Elena. She is a remarkable woman, a "good" person surely, but more significantly a woman interested in "active goodness." Her love affair with Insarov is therefore motivated by her sense of his great power for acting resolutely in the interests of an unimpeachable objective. As is true of Bazarov, one is left at Insarov's death with a sense of waste; but it is an acceptable caution against the hard-willed who defy death and seek to act as though they were immortal.

Turgenev saw more clearly than his contemporaries the genuinely human reasons for the Hamlet symbol in modern literature. The modern Hamlet decides against action because he is not able to bring a strong resolve to the problems he faces. There is a wide range of Hamlet figures in modern literature. At its comic extreme, he is the truly "superfluous man." In the field of tragedy, his end comes as a consequence of truly affecting agonies of the spirit. In *Virgin Soil* (1877),[9] Turgenev sets the tragic Hamlet Nezhdanov against a lesser revolutionary, Markelov. This latter, though he has many admirable qualities, is a truly perceptive study in the limitations of "authentic heroism." Markelov has a brutal strength of conviction which enables him to make the "heroic mistake." "Sincere, upright, a passionate and unhappy nature, he was capable at any moment of appearing merciless, bloodthirsty, of deserving to be called a monster, and was equally capable of sacrificing himself, without hesitation and without return." (*I*, 117–18)

Nezhdanov is another type, one of the most interesting Hamlet figures of modern literature, the more so because his final act is suicide. One may note super-ficially that his suicide shows a weakness of resolve, and surely Turgenev's critics so complained. But the act of suicide is one of the more interesting expres-sions of the self as hero; Nezhdanov's is one of many, though it is more truly a Hamlet gesture than any other. He is conscious of his Hamlet role from the be-ginning—not only of the indecisiveness, the lack of "pure resolve," but of what he calls "the loathsome enjoyment of one's own self-depreciation!" (*I, 198*) His suicide is a foregone conclusion, the ultimate act of indecision. It is, in the economy of suicide, a testi-mony of his sensitivity to an overwhelmingly complex and difficult human world. Turgenev's idea is sig-nificant. Nezhdanov's reason for suicide is that he sees too much, senses too much, to act with the nar-row and brutal simplicity of Markelov: "I could find no other way out of it. I could not *simplify myself*; the only thing left was to blot myself out altogether." (*II, 241*)

Nezhdanov's is one of three major types of suicide in modern literature. To take one's own life because one cannot "simplify" himself is to act from weak-ness in a sense, but primarily from an excessive aware-ness of weakness. Kirilov's suicide is an act of pure strength, though even here Dostoevsky shows that the quality of his act changes as it moves from the ab-stract thesis which is its original motive to the actual moment itself. Kirilov will kill himself to prove that he can do so; more than that, to defy the *fear of death*, which is the essential supporting motive of a belief in God. If he can take over the responsibility for his death, he will replace God. This is Dostoevsky's ulti-mate criticism of the social hero who assumes a per-sonal responsibility to demonstrate the perfectibility of man. All revolutionary heroes have a fraction of the same incentive; they will their deaths in adjusting to the danger of them. Malraux's Kyo (*Man's Fate*) translates himself beyond the role of victim by controlling his death (by a matter of minutes). There is one other type of suicide in the history of the modern self. He is the underground man who retreats to the ultimate "cave," "hole," "cellar," from motives of the ultimate despair, or merely from a sense of the absurdity of continuing. Dostoevsky's undergroundling does not go so far, and it is a part of Dostoevsky's strategy that he should not. In fact, the underground man of Dostoevsky's *Notes* is proud of his extraordinary mental division, of the "difference" and the distinction it affords him. He is not "average," rational, mediocre, expedient. The successors of Dostoevsky's anti-hero were neither so articulate nor so fortunate. In a majority of cases they committed suicide because circumstances permitted them to, or even demanded that they do so.

v

In Dostoevsky's fiction, all forms of self-expression are variants of the underground. The gamble his heroes take in their actions is a risk that Christ may not have existed—or, rather, that He too had been deceived and had suffered His crucifixion and death in the service of the "great lie." Once again Kirilov's behavior is very much to the point. He too sacrifices himself, but in defiance of the pattern of religious myth, not because he is uncertain or "too complex," but because he is representative man challenging the power of religious motive. Not only his act of suicide, but his discussion of it, the elaborate set of justifications he offers for it, are of the utmost importance to this study. For he offers his suicide as the ultimate expression of self-will.

I shall proclaim my self-will. I am bound to believe that I do not believe. I shall begin and end, and open the door. And I shall save. Only this will save mankind and will transform it physically in the next generation. For in his present physical condition man cannot . . . get along without his former God. For three years I've been searching for the attribute of my divinity, and I've found it: the attribute of my divinity is—Self-Will! [10]

This is of course absurd, but it is the ultimate expression of humanitarian sacrifice. Kirilov will suffer his death to prove that Christ's death was a self-deception. But of course neither act is absolutely guaranteed to be free of fundamental error. Dostoevsky presents Kirilov as an exaggerated demonstration of the extraordinary consequences of uninstructed self-will. So too Raskolnikov of *Crime and Punishment* has pushed the delusion of independent human power to a point of disaster. In every case other than Kirilov's, the spirit of Christ, in one form or another, returns to restore a sense of faith in His person as both divine and human.[11] Without Him, Dostoevsky's heroes are left in a perilous state, prey to their doubts. If they do not accept Christ, they are confronted with the devil whom they have invented to take Christ's place.

The crucial dramatic test in Dostoevsky's fiction has always to do with the balance, the admixture, the quality of fusion, of the divine and the human in Christ's nature. That balance is imperiled again and again, as Christ makes his way in Dostoevsky's world. There is always the terrible risk, which Kirilov translates into a naked challenge, that Christ is wholly man and not at all divine, that man has thoroughly corrupted Him. In these observations, and in their development in Dostoevsky's fiction, we have one of the truly important themes in modern literary views of mortality. As circumstances erode faith, the Christ figure becomes more and more human, and, as human, an emblematic or symbolic scapegoat victim. But the intimations of Godhood never entirely leave the figure of Christ. Some remnant of New Testament ritual adheres to even the most nonreligious expression.

Christ may be said in Dostoevsky to have struggled persistently against two major pressures in modern life: the force of self-will (that is, of merely irrational eccentricity), and the force of rational denial of the will. In the latter case we have the plotters of revolution, the pitiful Committees of Five; they are after all a major enemy of Dostoevsky's post-exile years. The other case, however, is less clear in Dostoevsky's examination of it. Most exhaustively in *Notes from the Underground*, Dostoevsky portrays the ambiguities of self-assertion as an indispensable act of humanity. One can think of the underground man as a minor, a comically overplayed Nezhdanov; Nezhdanov takes his life because he despairs of resolving his nature into a feasible and practical pattern of living; he cannot "simplify" himself. The underground man, however, is proud of his unsimple nature; it is a mark of self-identity, and it establishes him as forever immune to the temptations of mediocrity. But isolated self-will, at either the extreme of Kirilov or that of the underground man, is in itself a fatally eccentric power.

In one sense, Dostoevsky is saying in the *Notes* that man is *not* a hero. He is not rational, except for a very small fragment of his nature, and that is ordinarily an instrument of his worst instincts. Far from being a rational man, he is merely clever and shrewd and opportunistic. If the reason is admired extravagantly, man suffers from being deprived of the most important qualities of his will; and the reason itself, all but insanely intent upon proof and disproof, discredits the symbolic means at the disposal of the human will.

Notes from the Underground is more than an attack upon rationality; it is a portrayal of a weirdly eccentric, self-willed creature, whose every gesture is suspect because too elaborately staged to be genuine. The complicated opening section is not an "editorial" written to establish Dostoevsky's point of view, but a preparation and a defense of the narrator's career.[12] As such, however, Part One is one of the most exhaustive statements of underground rationale in all literature. The underground man is a "paradoxical fellow," as Dostoevsky calls him. Superficially, the idea is simple enough: He has free will and asserts the privilege of it against those who say man does not have it. He would therefore seem to have the power to choose what he shall do, and the range of possibility is extremely wide.

In a number of Dostoevsky's heroes, that choice is a formidable one. Ivan Karamazov, having chosen to renounce God, for his own failure to accept the slightest evidence of human brutality, has in consequence to attribute not only his but Smerdyakov's acts to his own willing. The most eloquently tense of Dostoevskian scenes testify to the agony of this privilege: Ivan's confronting the suicide of Smerdyakov; the moment of Kirilov's suicide, when the act itself is still necessary but the motive for it has become all but meaningless; Rogozhin and Myshkin facing each other in a moment of intense moral crisis. But our underground man will not permit a genuine crisis to occur. He is too much himself and double inextricably confused. In short, Dostoevsky's *Notes* presents us with only one of his many explorations of the painfully self-willed "superfluous man."

But the underground man is much too insignifi-

cantly "mean" in his assertions to be called more than
a pathetic creature at best; at worst he is meanly
comic, a Prufrock who prefers not to bathe, above all
a man given to the grossest pleasures in sentimental
violations of human decorum. The properties of the
modern hero are all here. The setting is the prototypi-
cal city, Petersburg, a labyrinth of narrow streets, of
rooms and halls, of darks and shadows and the grey
lines and streaks of an impoverished spirit. The city
isolates man from man; one has the impression in
most of Dostoevsky's fiction of isolated souls occasionally meeting, joining together, screaming hysteri-
cally over their loss of human contact.

In this world more than in any other the wall assumes its modern literary value. It is no longer a protective but has become a constricting force. The wall
of the *Notes* is the supreme end-product of the life of
reason, the narrator's small share of a Crystal Palace
of rationalist prophecy. That he should accept the
fact of the wall without allowing it to dominate his
will is to his credit. But the actual physical property of
wallness is the external manifestation of a personal,
psychological, even a "spiritual" condition. The underground man is *of* the wall, not only becomes
inured to it but makes it over through willing it to be a
reductive symbol of the world itself. It is not only that
the room, the flat, the "lodgings" of the underground
character are *there*, but that *he* is there *in them*: "I
carried the dark cellar about with me in my soul. I
was terribly afraid of being seen, of meeting someone
I knew, of being recognized." (153) [13]

In effect, the underground of the narrator is his soul,
the quality and character of his soul; it is the extreme
of ugly introspection. Instead of projecting beyond it,
he has *introjected*, finding in consciousness, in sensitivity, a value in itself, and thus welcoming the "dis-

ease" an over-reaching consciousness stimulates. Like Oblomov, the underground man withdraws from the external world: not because he fears it, however, but because he loathes it, because it damages his own self-esteem. He has retreated to the paltry, minuscule area of the inner self and it has misshaped him forever. To create a world is to assume others as well; the others in his case are mirror images of himself (or, on some occasions, himself listening to and watching himself), and "enemies." These latter are not in any real sense antagonists; they are instead indifferent persons reconstituted as enemies, people who because they would "just as soon" ignore him violate his self-pride.

Much needs to be read into the narrator's discussion of consciousness. "I assure you, gentlemen," he says, "that to be too acutely conscious is a disease, a real honest to goodness disease" (111). What he has in mind is the sensitivity to himself in terms of his surroundings, as well as an almost absurd sensitivity to the mirror reflection of his behavior and appearance. Abnormal sensitivity leads to inaction: "The direct, the inevitable, the legitimate result of consciousness is to make all action impossible, or—to put it differently —consciousness leads to thumb-twiddling" (122). This is in itself a form of egoism, a sense of superiority over those insensitive creatures who see things as "reasonable" and act "wisely" to accept them. The underground man distinguishes himself from them in his awareness of will and his pride of difference. If consciousness leads to suffering, he will accept suffering as a testimony of his uniqueness. "You see, gentlemen, reason is an excellent thing, there's no disputing that, but reason is nothing but reason and satisfies only the rational side of man's nature, while will is a manifestation of the whole life . . . I, for instance, quite naturally want to live, in order to satisfy all my capacities for life, and not simply my capacity for reasoning, that is, not simply one twentieth of my capacity for life." (133)

This is the underground man's free choice, and much is made of it by way of linking it to the "dreadful freedom" of the existentialist choice. There is much the same *initial* importance in the decision, but the undergroundling does not, as the total design of the *Notes* clearly proves, choose in the sense of Camus' absurd man, but rather chooses to be different from those who insult him by ignoring them. Throughout those scenes of the *Notes* that are a form of perverted Rousseauistic memoir, his actions are spiteful and hateful and the very reverse of honest admissions of self. These ambiguities should surely suggest that the *Notes* does not simply defend the advantages of self-will. Dostoevsky is treating its anti-hero in somewhat the same way as Ezra Pound treats Hugh Selwyn Mauberley. He is in short damning his enemies but also damning his hero—who while different from his enemies is not himself validly acceptable.

vi

Surely, Ivan's challenge to Alyosha in the Grand Inquisitor scene of *The Brothers Karamozov* is not answered there. Nor is it ever answered logically in Dostoevsky's fiction. There are persons who seem "on the edge" of answering it: Christ himself, who kisses the Grand Inquisitor and leaves him; Father Zossima, whose sanctity inspires others to confess; Alyosha, whose acts of forbearance are like those of Christ himself; the two simple prostitutes, Sonia and Lisa, who seem Christ's delegated servants on this earth; above all, Prince Myshkin, who timidly mediates between extremes of evil in *The Idiot*.

The challenge is simply this: that Christ had chosen to present man with the gift of self-will, which he does not know how to use, and had therefore caused much suffering. "Without a clear idea of what to live for man will not consent to live and will rather destroy himself than remain on the earth, though he were surrounded by loaves of bread. That is so, but what became of it? Instead of gaining possession of men's freedom, you gave them greater freedom than ever! Or did you forget that a tranquil mind and even death is dearer to man than the free choice in the knowledge of good and evil?" [14]

The Inquisitor has frankly acceded to man's terror, his wish to abandon the gift of freedom, and has in turn presented him with peace and bread. In this sense, that freedom of choice involves a moral responsibility, and that man is driven mad trying to associate his will with the economy of evil in the world, the underground man had rightly claimed consciousness as a disease. In setting up the Grand Inquisitor as Christ's antagonist, Ivan has himself taken over the responsibility of God's will; he has exalted man above God and proposed a temporal society to govern and quiet the disturbances of the will. But of course Christ and the Devil, the principal active metaphors of God's will on earth, are complementary extensions of man's will into infinity. Both Christ and the Devil appear in Dostoevsky in plain clothes and with the marks of corruption upon them. They are, in a really important sense, Dostoevsky's major literary figures. Having banished Christ in the Grand Inquisitor scene, Ivan is not long thereafter visited by His complementary spirit, also a product of his imagination.

Dostoevsky thought often about the precise character of man's immortal condition; that it was indispensable he had no doubt, but he nevertheless found it very difficult to believe in. He lived always in the agonized necessity of accepting a truth that it was all but impossible to believe. When a correspondent asked him just what form or appearance the immortal spirit would assume at the resurrection, he speculated that it would not appear as the mortal body, but rather like the body of Christ between His resurrection and ascension. It is at that moment that Christ's body—assuredly His face—would most strongly testify to the hazards of corporeality. The pattern of Dostoevsky's defense of the will is most clearly in the line of these observations. He frequently manifested the profound influence his narrow escape from death had had upon him—not only the escape itself, but the expectation of the death he had missed. The moment before death seemed to have a special, a mystic quality, providing an insight above all insights into the life hereafter; and the moment of illumination before the loss of consciousness in an attack of epilepsy seemed the experience that most nearly resembled it.

The consciousness of man is a period of painful awareness between two others, about which speculation is difficult. This is the meaning of the captious remark the underground man makes, that "consciousness is a disease," and that pain is a sign of awareness. Surely no man experienced pain more intensely than Christ; to no one was the experiencing of human consciousness at once so much a sacrifice and so extraordinary a means of human salvation. But, as he struggled his lifetime over the question of immortality, Dostoevsky was never sure that Christ might not after all have been merely human, or that He had renounced His divinity as a consequence of the painful experiencing of His humanity.

Dostoevsky's writings often betray a condition of

wariness, of being "on guard" against evidences of corruption. There is no pure spirit in Dostoevsky, no saint who is free of the "breath of corruption." The stench of the corpse assails both the body and the spirit. What is to guarantee that man is immortal? If Christ is that guarantee, for He was man and is God, how can we be sure that Kirilov was not after all correct, that He was after all deceived, like the rest of us? Since Dostoevsky could not tolerate the arrogance of a Godless freedom of will (those of his heroes who express it kill themselves or go mad from the moral burden of their own assertions), Christ becomes his single major hero, the only protagonist of the human self in the question of its sharing or reflecting divinity.

A central fact in Dostoevsky's career was the experience of seeing, in the Basel museum, Hans Holbein's paintings, of Christ taken from the Cross and of the entombment.

> He stood for twenty minutes before the picture without moving [his wife reports]. On his agitated face was the frightened expression I often noticed on it during the first moments of his epileptic fits. He had no fit at the time, but he could never forget the sensation he had experienced in the Basel museum in 1867: the figure of Christ taken from the cross, whose body already showed signs of decomposition, haunted him like a horrible nightmare.[15]

The painting is one of a series called "The Passion of Christ"; in it the humanity of Christ—that is, of his body—is fully manifest. The face is distended to show the agony recently endured on the cross. The bruises and stains of the punishment are given in relentless realism. Most important to Dostoevsky are the signs of the body's decomposition. Many impressions must have gone through his mind: the memory of his own narrow escape; his continuous interest thereafter in the appearance of those condemned and at the moment of their death; most of all, the overbearing wonder and doubt that must have haunted him: Can this creature be God? All divinity seems to have fled Him; is not man's cruelty so powerful that it can destroy His divinity forevermore? If this be possible, then we must surely surrender our fate to the Kirilovs and Verhovenskys of this world?

In the background of Holbein's painting is an open cave, an "underground," the tomb to which Christ's disciples are bringing him. Also in the Basel museum is a painting of "Christ in the Tomb." Here the process of decomposition has advanced a bit; the flesh wounds of the crucifixion are exaggerated as the fleshly covering has receded. It is this state, this condition, which Dostoevsky speculatively assigns to the human body upon its resurrection. It requires an almost impossible exercise of the imagination to assume either divinity or humanity in it. But the hazard that divinity is a triumph over humanity at the moment when the latter seems least "healthy" or promising or prepossessing is at the source of Dostoevsky's thought. The suggestion haunts the characterization of the underground man in modern literature. It is not only that sickness and sensitivity go together (Mann, Kafka), but that a state of robust health seems to contravene the desiderata of suffering that force men toward the condition of the entombed divinity.

The Holbein painting dominates the milieu of *The Idiot* (1869). This novel brings into focus several of Dostoevsky's underground speculations. There is the underground scene of Petersburg, never (except perhaps in *Crime and Punishment*) so brilliantly evoked: The Ivolgin house is especially alive with undergroundling animation. Beyond this, and lacking (though, as we understand, "censored" out of Chapter IX) in the *Notes,* is the figure of Holbein's Christ and its active humanization in the character of Prince Myshkin. That he is a "Prince" has its obvious implications as well as its small ironic effects.

Myshkin is not only the Dostoevsky of the twenty minutes before the Holbein painting. He is also, in a quite thoroughly transmuted form, the Christ of that painting. He may also be the image of Dostoevsky as Christ. At any rate, Myshkin speculates much upon the painting, upon suffering, and upon death. He had observed a guillotining in Lyons, and offers a vivid report of the experience to the Epanchin sisters. "Just now when you asked me for a subject for a picture," he tells Adelaida, "it occurred to me to tell you to paint the face of a condemned man a minute before the fall of the guillotine blade, when he is still standing on the scaffold and before he lies down on the plank." (*The Idiot, p.* 90)

When he is pressed for an explanation, he refers to the painting at Basel; the face of the condemned Christ becomes the image of all men momentarily expecting death. While Holbein's Christ expresses primarily the tortures of the moments before death, Dostoevsky, through his Prince, reads into His face the pain of uncertainty, the agony of mortality on the edge of a region of the greatest doubt of all. Myshkin acts out, in scene after scene, this moment of doubt. The doubts of Myshkin—of his sanity, his strength of mind and strength of character—are pale reflections of the major doubt of immortality itself, and of man's deserving it. This is held in suspension throughout the novel, and is finally indulged in the ghastly concluding scene: The body of Nastasya Filippovna, murdered by Rogozhin, lies there covered with a white sheet. The Prince and Rogozhin move toward it, but the Prince halts, as Dostoevsky must have halted before the painting, in crucial meditation: "The prince looked, and he felt that the longer he looked the more still and death-like the room became. Suddenly a fly, awakened from its sleep, started buzzing, and after flying over the bed, settled at the head of it. The prince gave a start." (652)

This moment still leaves Dostoevsky's meditations without conclusion, concerning the role of Christ. Nastasya, who was "in the care of" Myshkin, in the sense that her fate depended upon her seeing him and believing in his purity of will, is dead nevertheless. Rogozhin, the murderer, who is Dostoevsky's complementary Devil to Myshkin's Christ, has been allowed to assert his power of evil. And the scene of the bedroom is a final testimony of the Prince's failure to arrest mortality. The noxious insect, the fly, is materialism incarnate, the *insect* to which all of literature's underground men are subsequently to revert. It is a terrifying scene, and it is brilliantly a projection of Dostoevsky's "frightened expression" before the Basel painting.

Terentyev, in many ways an unpleasant reminder of the underground man, has seen a copy of the Holbein painting in Rogozhin's house. In the document, "Necessary Explanation," offered an assemblage of Myshkin's friends, he expresses on a lesser level, the revolts of Kirilov and Ivan Karamazov. But his observations concerning the painting are of more than ordinary interest. If such a corpse had been seen by Christ's disciples, he says, "then how could they possibly have believed, as they looked at the corpse, that that face and that body represented a Being that had been designed to signal the triumph of man over death"; and yet, "Looking at that picture, you get the impression of nature as some enormous, implacable, and dumb beast, or, to put it more correctly, as some huge engine of the latest design, which has senselessly seized, cut to pieces, and swallowed up—impassively and unfeelingly—a great and priceless Being, a Being worth the whole of nature and its laws, worth the entire earth, which was perhaps created solely for the coming of that Being!" (447) [16]

This is not merely a diatribe against the cruelty of man and his moral misadventures, but still another statement of the doubt, from which no Dostoevsky character is excused, of the capacity of that "Being" to conquer mortality. Myshkin most fully dramatizes that doubt, which Terentyev after all has only superficially verbalized; it is compounded in every experience the Prince has with the look of evil—in the face of Rogozhin as he encounters it before his first attack of epilepsy, but most poignantly in the portrait of Nastasya, even before he has seen her personally. "I looked at *her face!* That morning even—I mean, when I looked at her portrait, I could not bear it." (626) Nastasya is mad; she is doomed. Myshkin cannot save her; he can take the blows intended for other victims, he can show in his own face the agonies and the tensions of others; but he cannot literally save others from what they will their fate to be.

The question that haunted Dostoevsky, and that continues to haunt writers who speculate upon the isolated figure of Christ in the modern landscape, has essentially to do with this passivity of Christ's role. It is a matter of the degree to which Christ, suffering increasingly the burden of men's sins, can absorb it without ceasing to be divine altogether. In this sense Christ Himself becomes the stereotype of the marginal self. His great gift is His sensitivity to human pain; His role is to translate that gift, by experiencing pain, into an essential sacrifice of Himself. If this act remains a master stroke of scapegoat artistry, it will preserve men from their own stubborn refusal to merit immortality. But Dostoevsky was bewildered by the all too human face of the Holbein Christ, and he could not allow his Myshkin to survive as a "positively good man" the exigencies of death, symbolized by the hovering fly over Nastasya's dead face. From this point forward, into twentieth-century literature and its histories of violence, the figure of Christ becomes more and more a companion-victim, a fellow-self on the margins of violence, elevated momentarily by Faulkner into an illusion of recaptured divinity, but human nonetheless, and without much conviction of His role as liaison between culpable man and the prospect of immortality.

vii

In the century since Dostoevsky's *Notes from the Underground*, there have been three principal literary metaphors of the marginal self: the Christ figure, already vividly presented in *The Idiot* and elsewhere; the underground man himself, who was to experience many interesting mutations in modern literature; and the clown, to whose general image one may add that of the poet, the artist, the acrobat, the juggler, and who in any case seems often relied upon to preserve a rhythm, a décor, a quality of life, that risks extinction.

As Robert Jackson[17] demonstrates, the underground man followed very closely the imagery and setting originally proposed by Dostoevsky. The characters of minor Russian novelists before 1917 live in "disgusting holes"; they are minor "Hamlets" who find their indecision sufficient unto the need; they set up a hostile dualism of sensitive soul versus clod; they discourse on night, darkness, and the impenetrability of walls; and, with rare exception, they commit suicide.

The fiction of Leonid Andreyev is closest to achieving a useful adaptation of the underground milieu. He is almost entirely without the suggestion, clear enough in Dostoevsky, that the underground is necessarily a place from which man should be rescued. Andreyev's men occupy rooms, cellars, prison cells, as finalities and not as refuges. The Andreyev hero flees the world and hides in the underground, sometimes to the point of willing a state of total passivity. "At every sound speaking of life he seemed to himself to be huge and unveiled, and he hugged himself together all the tighter and silently groaned—neither with voice nor in thought—since he feared now his own voice and his own thoughts. He prayed to someone that the day might not come so that he might always lie under the heap of rags, without movement or thought." ("In the Basement," 1901)

This move toward inanition is of interest not because of the peculiarities of its Russian background, but for its suggestions of what is to come in twentieth-century literature. There is a very definite line of development in it of withdrawal from a world that becomes increasingly glaring and noisy; Hermann Hesse's *Steppenwolf* (1929) is in part a testimony of that tradition. But beyond that, the move in modern literature toward a complete renewal of all questions of humanity accompanies the career of underground literature. In short, because of outward violence or inner desire, human society and the human being himself are cut down to almost minimum mortal limits— even, on occasion, transformed into nonhuman figures who testify in a weirdly new fabulist literature to the status of human reduction.

In addition to these variants of underground literature, one needs to acknowledge the role of prison literature, particularly in death-house scenes, in which
the entire quality of the walled-in society is overwhelmingly dominated by the expectations of death.
Brendan Behan's *The Quare Fellow* (1956) and Jean
Genet's *The Death Watch* (1949) come immediately
to mind. In this case the wall, so familiar an underground image, becomes quite strictly and accurately
the boundary line between life and death. In Behan's
play, the litanies of a religion from "beyond the wall"
strive vainly to preserve the sense of a transition to an
immortal life, but the prison routine has quite thoroughly eroded the promise. The wall of a prison or a
jail cell can easily be said to represent almost what it
literally and physically is: an impenetrable block of
stone or steel, shutting off the consciousness from all
customary experience. In the work of Jean-Paul
Sartre, the wall *becomes* mortality itself; it spatially
cuts off the horizon, and in the same sense indicates a
cessation of all time. Since the possibilities of the
existentialist ego are entirely dependent upon its projection into future time, the wall starkly prohibits further self-definition.

One of the most important observations of the modern view of self concerns its move toward reduction
and limitation. This is of course closely related to its
loss of sensed value, to put it simply, the disappearance of self-confidence. The line of descent follows
along the path leading from immortality to the
closed-in, reduced, minimum view of mortality. The
effect upon literature is to make scene and temporal
effects closely coincident; there is a corresponding
shift in types of symbolism.

To take two of the most important symbols, associated with Dostoevsky's underground man: the walls

of the rented room become spatial limits, within which the self can almost be said to move only inwardly; the self is itself correspondingly reduced and demeaned. These symbolic circumstances dominate modern literary meditations upon the character and quality of the self. The wall is seen more and more as an insuperable barrier, an obstacle to self-assertion, except in the extraordinary circumstance, frequently mocked in modern literature, when it becomes the limit of an introspective universe. To it are added the mirror images, which multiply and fractionate the self, so that one self becomes many fragments, in close-order duplication of itself.

The character of the self is correspondingly reduced. Dostoevsky's underground anti-hero on several occasions contemptuously refers to his "enemy's" regard for him as an insect, a low form of animal matter; the bureaucratic self of Dostoevsky's contemporaries struggles against this kind of self-estimate. Clothes are the key to esteem, as in another form they are signs of degradation. As the figure of the underground man is taken over in twentieth-century literature, clothes become covering, an accurate external sign of a basic self-estimate.

The contraction of the self is frequently described in terms of the circumstances of escape, of hiding from a formidable authority, or of withdrawal into impenetrable securities of fantasy, dream, madness. Not only do the images of "cave," "cellar," "cage," "shell" increase. Since the self has become a refuge from the nonself, from an inexplicable, a domineering "father," it assumes the several roles of the scurrying animal or insect, hiding both itself from the view of the outside and its own view from itself. Ultimately this reductive process re-creates the entire, extensive scope of problems concerning self-knowledge. In its extreme cases, the reduced self suffers the complex and confusing responsibility of self-determination on the most primitive and most unsophisticated levels of insight and outlook.

Kafka's heroes are undoubtedly the most interesting modern variants of this self-reduction. His remarkable skill in presenting the minutiae of a setting suggests a realistic miniaturist, who moves closer and closer to an object until its character and its action are observed almost without perspective. This manipulation of details is accompanied by another type of representation of equal importance: the fragmenting of universals, so that they are seen within the strange perspectives of part-selves, conscious and conscientious within a quite inadequate range of perception. Kafka employs these techniques as a means of representing a kind of literary meditation that is like Dostoevsky's and yet very much unlike it.

The essential difference is rhetorical. Kafka's selves speak softly—or, if they shout, they are immediately aware of the intrusive strength of their voices. They scurry; they are "busy" beyond all conception of busyness; their pride leads not to major dramatic tensions —as in Dostoevsky's principal scenes—but to strange, timid, odd projections of the ego. The Kafkan hero is above all sensitive of his insignificance; he acts out his unimportance by reducing his size, spatial range of movement, relationship to the objects around him, conscientious regard for a massive, deep, inexplicable authority. As he reduces himself, the space in which he lives loses its rational significations. Sounds which were formerly rational speech split the air; hallways which once were precise lines of motion become maze-like and confusing; there is a corresponding failure of communication with the nonself, the "others," who react to gestures strangely and unpredictably. Finally, there is a fundamental change in self-regard. The self comes to *expect* that it will diminish or change its shape, exaggerating certain motions, and otherwise enduring the displacement of the dream life.

Kafka's "Metamorphosis" [18] is the best example of these forms of self-reduction. Gregor Samsa literally *becomes* what he had at times feared he was—an insect image of his own fear of self-servitude. At the same time he is incredulous concerning the change. Lying in bed, he tries to arise from it, thinking always of his "obligations" to the world that has found the metamorphosis; but the very form to which he has reverted is designed to defeat all efforts conscientiously to obey that world. He has become legs and soft underbelly, and shell: "He would have needed arms and hands to hoist himself up; instead he had only the numerous little legs which never stopped waving in all directions and which he could not control in the least." (*p.* 71)

The subsequent history of Gregor Samsa is a remarkable progress in self-degradation. The insect he has become exerts all of its energy in seeking spaces to accommodate its withdrawal. Gregor's self-estimation flares up and dies, and it is crushed absolutely by virtue of now having become entirely dependent on whimsical tolerance. The transformation of the underground man is almost complete. He is no longer privileged to alternate resentful hiding with aggressive assertion; nor is he able except fitfully to pretend to human selfhood. The bewilderment of his parents turns quickly to resentful hostility, then to disbelief, finally to relief that the remains of selfhood have disappeared altogether. Gregor ends with the unceremonious disposal of his insect body. "It did not take [the Charwoman] long to establish the truth of the matter, and her eyes widened, she let out a whistle, yet did not waste much time over it but tore open the door of the Samsas' bedroom and yelled into the darkness at the top of her voice: 'Just look at this, it's dead; it's lying here dead and done for!'" (128)

This story of the total disintegration of the self has several aspects of importance. It represents, for one thing, a complete reversion to passivity. In this connection, the self does not "enjoy" observing its condition, nor can it physically do anything to improve it. Gregor does make a few adventurous journeys outside his room, but he soon becomes aware of his totally repulsive appearance and character; and he willingly cooperates with his sister in keeping himself from view. The story also suggests an abject resignation to irrational authority. It is not only the father who represents that authority, but the mysterious natural forces responsible for the metamorphosis itself. In any final judgment, these natural forces are within Gregor himself. His rational aggressions, in the earlier role of commercial traveler, have induced caricature states and gestures, which have in this half-willed, half-accidental metamorphosis been translated into their animal surrogates.

Kafka's portrayal of underground man marks a clear development beyond Dostoevsky's, but it has its precedents in the preoccupation of such writers as Andreyev with the special effects of underground décor. A steady progress in limitation is noted in this examination of the modern self. The symbolic properties of the underground life seem to have the strength of renewal and perpetuation. The spatial limitations become in themselves spiritual restrictions. Self-concern over position, status, distinction, jealousies and resentments, these have the inevitable consequence of reducing the scale of self-relationships until, in an absolute sense, the self becomes unique. But this uniqueness is at the antipolar extreme from that of the Emersonian self. The underground self becomes uniquely nothing, or the next thing to nothing.

It is true that Kafka also portrays certain adventures in self-assertion, but these are always—or seem to be —designed to suggest a last-chance expression of individuality. "A Hunger Artist," for example, is in one reading of it a caricature of self-pride, an assertion of uniqueness. There is pride of "profession" involved; the hunger artist would want it known that he is a master of self-denial; but of course he confesses at the end that he had made an art of fasting because "I couldn't find the food I liked." This caricature of self-assertion is interesting for its having carried the human inclination to martyrdom to its extremity. The martyr in this case dies of starvation, but his sacrifice is not credible; nor does he have an audience to admire or profit from it. In a sense, the hunger artist marks a conceivable end of the passive Christ. In the room where Nastasya's dead body lies, Myshkin reverts to idiocy. His virtues had always been passive ones, and it is to be assumed that the idiocy to which he turns at the novel's end will be a caricature of passivity. The hunger artist is the end-result of that caricature. His "performance" is clearly a parody of the piéta, as Robert W. Stallman has pointed out.[10] Note, for example, the manager's handling of him before his audience:

> The impresario came forward, without a word—for the band made speech impossible—lifted his arms in the air above the artist, as if inviting Heaven to look down upon its creature here in the straw, this suffering martyr, which indeed he was, although in quite another sense; grasped him round the emaciated waist, with exaggerated caution, so that the frail condition he was in might

be appreciated; and committed him to the care of the blenching ladies, not without secretly giving him a shaking so that his legs and body tottered and swayed.[20]

As the "Metamorphosis" marks the extreme to which the underground man's withdrawal from authority could go, so "A Hunger-Artist" is in one sense a caricature of the sententious assumption that suffering is in itself a pledge of self-transcendence. For here the display of suffering, so conspicuously successful in Holbein's portrayal of the Christ, becomes a thing in itself without either the external virtue of influence or the internal satisfaction of self-pride.

viii

The significance of the underground man as a symbol of the marginal self achieves its final position in the nonheroes of Samuel Beckett's novels and plays. What were in Dostoevsky's time discernible and identifiable objects in a milieu (reduced in number and importance, but still part of an inventory) become in Beckett reductive and limited arbiters of space manipulation. Here, in a room or in an open spaceway, the self as object maneuvers spatially from a shifting center, pondering and querying its significance, in effect trying to resolve the minimal doubts of existence itself.

One needs to reflect upon the degree to which the human self has in this literature reduced its confidence. Beckett's creatures say much about "being at the center," and they warn themselves of the dangers of being off-center; but their center is actually purely a spatial one, the very reversal of the Emersonian projective ego. The following passage in The Unnamable [21] is an expression of what we may call epistemological timidity; it does not assert center but inquires about spatial relationships as a *sine qua non* condition of existence.

> I like to think I occupy the center, but nothing is less certain. In a sense I would be better off at the circumference, since my eyes are always fixed in the same direction. . . . From center to circumference in any case it is a far cry and I may well be situated somewhere between the two. . . . But the best is to think of myself as fixed and at the center of this place, whatever its shape and extent may be. (*pp.* 406–7)

These are the spatial minima necessary if one is even to speak of himself as an object capable of penetrating a limited range of matter that is not itself. In one of his "versions," the creature of this novel, without arms or legs, is situated within a huge pot outside a third-rate restaurant. It has eyes (though these are defective, and they seem unable to stop a flow of what are apparently tears); there is some doubt that it has hearing; it is not otherwise self-sustaining and must be occasionally moved in and out of its residence. There is of course an "unnamable" past. "They," presumably educators, parents, lawmakers and ministers, have at some time or other given him "the low-down on God. They told me I depended on him, in the last analysis." There were also "fellow-creatures," but all of this is quite vague, and anyway these others were full of poison it is good now to be rid of. The past is arbitrarily dismissible, and it is even not really credible, since it cannot be spatially comprehended. As for the future, the Unnamable wants some assurance that he has lived before he will die.

> It is certain I was grievously mistaken in supposing that death in itself could be regarded as evidence, or even a strong presumption, in support of a preliminary life. And I for my part have no longer the least desire to

leave this world, in which they keep trying to foist me, without some kind of assurance that I was really there, such as a kick in the arse, for example, or a kiss, the nature of the attention is of little importance, provided I cannot be suspected of being its author. (475)

The soul turns in its "cage," as another Beckett creature, Malone, says, "as in a lantern, in the night without haven or craft or matter or understanding." [22] The gamble of existence comes down to the matter of testing one's ability to "come and go"—or, if not that, one's skill in seeing an object in spatial relation to oneself. The universe has come back to a room within range of sight, hearing, and smell. Space is pre-eminent and essential to selfhood, but here only to survival, or perhaps even to the barest *sense* of what it is to exist. Beckett's underground man has long since given up posturing, maintaining an attitude, hating or resenting. Instead, he follows the downward path of disintegration. Legs fall, arms disappear, eyelids cease to function, and the room elides imperceptibly into a condition of tomb. The light, if it exists at all, is a dim gray, seeping through a small high window, beyond which there is nothing of which the self may be sure.

The play *Endgame* [23] provides a parody of the self's former power of creation. Its central figure, Hamm, is in a wheel chair, in which he essays several journeys "'round the world." He is blind. His parents, Nagg and Nellie, are in trash cans, out of which their heads occasionally pop, in which they "die"—that is, they cease their limited awareness of their being in space. "Take me for a little turn," Hamm says to his attendant, Clov, "Right round the world!" "Hug the walls, then back to the center again." "I was right in the center, wasn't I?" (25–26) Hamm, as are other Beckett figures, is victim of a twin disaster. He is certainly a creature suffering the effects of violence—so that we may rightly suspect that the world beyond the small square of window does not exist. But he is also the extreme end-product of his willing nonexistence, if only to assert his power of will. Like Dostoevsky's underground man, he is anxious to assure himself that there is a being definable as himself. But there is no design of reference to which he cares to attend; the world as such does not exist, except that, in his wheel chair, he is "at the center" of a space arbitrarily limited to his capacity of motion.

Beckett's work is a half-mocking, half-sympathetic meditation on what he calls "our pernicious and incurable optimism." This optimism is a will-to-live, which in the form presented here is reduced to a kind of fluid persistence through changing lights and shadows. The circumstances are almost incredibly forbidding; they sometimes reduce themselves to the faintest shreds of sensual evidence. Yet, as Beckett remarks, "The individual is the seat of a constant process of decantation, decantation from the vessel containing the fluid of future time, sluggish, pale and monochrome, to the vessel containing the fluid of past time, agitated and multicolored by the phenomena of its hours." [24] The process would seem at best only mildly amusing, were it not for the fact that, in conditions disastrously formidable, man ceaselessly questions the terms of his selfhood as he proceeds to final negation.

In an ultimate sense, the phenomenon of self inhabiting a space which alters in form, color, and light according to some preordained design reduces itself to a condition of waiting. Waiting involves enduring, filling in the hours and noting their passage, suffering the boredom which the living seems to require. It is perhaps appropriate that Beckett's most notorious character should not appear at all—that, in any definable sense, he should not even exist. Godot, in any traditional frame of reference, is God; but, according to any precise terms of credibility, God does not exist. He is nonexistent in the sense that He does not and will not appear. Estragon and Vladimir are obliged to wait for Him, to expect Him; but they are responsible for their own being, for tolerating the shifts and changes in the shape and color of their surroundings. In short, they must exist and are their only reliable agents of self-continuance. In these circumstances, each of them is tyrant, critic, actor and spectator, and Christ. The Christ figure is wholly shorn of divinity; there seems no link between Estragon and Godot, unless Estragon is himself the Christ, now entirely human.

VLADIMIR   But you can't go barefoot!
ESTRAGON   Christ did.
VLADIMIR   Christ! What has Christ got to do with it? You're not going to compare yourself to Christ!
ESTRAGON   All my life I've compared myself to him.
VLADIMIR   But where he lived it was warm, it was dry!
ESTRAGON   Yes. And they crucified quick.
    Silence [25]

Waiting for Godot is a complete, skeletonized, miniature history of the human self. Estragon and Vladimir are underground-hobo-clown reductions of maximum self-power. All phases of self-pretense are contained within the play. Belief in God is now reduced to a "filling in" and a tolerating of hours and days, a waiting for a nonexisting or an imprecisely visioned Godot. Godot is himself authority of whatever kind in which the comic heroes place a hesitant and unknowing trust. Theology is represented in the cacophony of Lucky's remarkable "sermon" about the nature of God and perfection; echoes of all portentous affirmations assault the air ("Given the existence as

uttered forth in the public works of Puncher and Wattmann of a personal God quaquaquaqua with white
beard quaquaquaqua time without extension . . ."
etc., (*p. 28*). Human cruelty, and a few of its manifestations in drives toward power, are acted out in the
two appearances of Pozzo and Lucky. Above all, the
play shows its two principals as comically and pathetically inept, though aware of the need to persist in
time, to remain statically and repetitiously themselves. Their strength lies in their "waiting," in their
having been—not without some small suggestion of
heroic endurance—responsible for the continuance of
themselves.

If *Waiting for Godot* is an existentialist play, surely
Estragon and Vladimir are existentialist heroes of a
very low temperature. They can scarcely be said to
participate in any "drama of existence." They are
pretty well reconciled at play's end to the necessity of
"waiting" without hope of Godot's arrival, and in that
sense they are "self-aware," responsible egos. But
theirs is no real *determination* to exist in the new
sense of assuming the "dreadful freedom" of their
choice of futures. They do not enforce existence, but
merely suffer it. And on these terms, they mark the
end-of-the-line, *"fin de partie"* consequence of the
undergroundling self. They are miracles of passivity,
possessed of what Beckett has called a "pernicious and
incurable optimism."

The terms of the self's history have invariably depended upon the two kinds of strength available to
the human personality: the quality and power of the
will and the special circumstances in which the self
at any time existed. A sense of vast and even endless
space seems to make the self a liberal and liberating
agent of existence. When the ratio of self to space
diminishes, changes occur in the self; its power of self-

will is indulged, becomes distorted, warped, and even wholly demented. There is a crucial point in the history of self when a hypothetical balance between inner and outer reality is upset, a crisis which Dostoevsky represents with a special brilliance in *Notes from the Underground*. The consequences of this imbalance are almost wholly inward. Indeed, the design of self occupying space is turned into a hundred weird distortions of both: Self may be so demeaned or so distrustful of its power as to become literally the fantasy creature it has used for defense; space is comparably reduced as the self's power to project beyond its center diminishes. In the end we have Beckett's creatures forced to a primitive renewal of the basically simple questions of origin, position and relation.

There is one other important element of this history. The self's imagination both conceptually and imagistically supports its claim to position and describes the way and the power of transcendence. Immortality is after all an extension of the self's will to continue, to remain superior to process. It is the primary "Godot" desideratum of the self's history. From the demands it makes, several images of authority, divinity, and transcendence emerge. But the moral ambiguities of a single, responsible God force the creation of the Christ image, who is less formidably divine and more authentically human. In the career of the Christ figure the self's last chance of overcoming mortality resides. The Christ moves with the variegations of the human fate from the center of His divinity to the blind end of His humanity, retaining consistently a quality of passive virtue, needed to absorb the blows the modern self has suffered. In twentieth-century literature, the Christ figure has usually tended to turn altogether human, or to become a superior clown. In either case, He stands out from the human cluster only in being especially designated to communicate the terrible distresses of marginality, even perhaps to help man to bear them, in a special kind of pathetic humor. He may of course altogether disappear, and has, in the wholly circumstantially antisentimental literature of such persons as Ionesco, Adamov, Genet, and in some of Beckett's works. In any case, the time seems very long ago indeed when the Dostoevskian character could so intensely and with so vivid a sense of personal power evoke both Christ and God as near conspirators in the self's adventures. We are similarly remote from the Emersonian image of the self, which while scarcely as intense, also called witness to the creation as joint product and responsibility of God and self.

CRITICS HAVE OFTEN SPECULATED upon Beckett's work
as an elaborate, destructive satire of the Enlightenment. Beckett joins Dostoevsky in the spirit of the
latter's rebellion against the "Westernism" of Turgenev, but most of all in his distrust of machinery, reason, and the planes and cubes of geometry. Beckett's
hero is less melodramatic, in many ways less given to
complex "performances" of his doubts and fears; he is
more strictly in line of descent from the major intellectual sponsors of *L'Éclaircissement*, but it is a *descent* in no uncertain terms.

Literary manners and techniques, particularly in the
novel, have had the appearance of a steady reduction
of auctorial scope and confidence. The envelope of social circumstance shrinks. The author gives in to his
characters, lets them have their way, and is finally reduced to the stratagem of permitting them their
doubts and building what theme is left upon elemen-
tally simple speculations about place, location, and
self-relations. The development is down from bold
metaphysical assertion to epistemological uncertainties. The narrative point of view is similarly changed.

Beckett occupies a curiously ambiguous position in
his analyses of self. His novels and plays are in one
sense solidly traditional: In their preoccupations with
self-definition, they invoke a language of careful and

even arduous inquiry; they are precise almost beyond the decent limits of precision. This does not mean that they are comprehensibly structured, or that their concerns are easily associated with matters of traditional fiction. The problems are themselves obsessively traditional; the manner of presentation is not.

Before we explore the relationship of literary techniques to the problems of the "vanishing self," we might determine just what these problems are. Roughly, they are divisible into two major classes of inquiry, metaphysical and epistemological; at some points in the history of literature, notably when literary criticism becomes more important than its subject-matter, these two kinds of investigation combine in a form of ontological query: That is, the matter of autonomous values in the artifact becomes primary and is independent of extra-aesthetic conventions.

Pre-eminently, the first metaphysical problem has to do with the existence and character of God. It is inevitably followed by the concern of man to determine the conditions according to which He may be known. The most important metaphysical question has to do with the *structure* of God's nature—that is, the forms of His accessibility to the human consciousness. How may an infinite being be known by a finite one, without either damaging His infinity or confusing finite impressions with the specifications of the absolute? These matters are never satisfactorily concluded, but lead only to compromises about which intuition, dogma, and "faith" are often fitfully arranged.

In the transition from the metaphysical to the epistemological grounds of literary speculation, a host of conventions are used. A middle ground is assumed; it is structured in terms of literary conventions that are halfway related to social custom, halfway founded upon taste. They are often a curious mixture of social and moral confidences. But they do assume aesthetic control. The author predominates; he is "in charge of" the manners and conventions according to which an invented consciousness relates to others within an imagined whole. All nineteenth-century novels presume this leading auctorial role, as do many twentieth-century novels. The author "speaks for God"; he settles upon the conditions in which God is assumed, and the moral conventions are viable and effectual.

In one of the most acute recent studies of narrative point of view, Norman Friedman speaks of "the disappearance of the author" as a major development in modern literature.[1] If this phrase has any significance, it is because it helps to define the shift from a metaphysical to an epistemological center in twentieth-century fiction. If we consider the metaphysical questions I have stated above, we will find that they have all but disappeared in modern literature; or, if they still exist, they do so only as hypotheses almost devoid of a sustaining confidence in their proof. The author "disappears," and is replaced either by the scene or by the consciousnesses of his personages. That is, he communicates obliquely; as a superintending and "felt" personality, he scarcely exists at all. His absence has almost always been thought by modern critics to be a testimony of his "skill"; self-effacement is considered a great aesthetic achievement. The author gives in to the scene, which is the ground of his art; or he explores the consciousnesses of his creatures, but remains—as *himself*—scrupulously outside of them.

Whether or not this tendency is a move toward a finer, purer "art," it seems surely to testify to a new philosophical conditioning of literature. One way of regarding the author's disappearance is to suggest a diminished structural confidence, a decline in shared metaphysical values. Interest in literary consciousness, when it isn't a confession of uncertainty concerning the power of generalization, results from a willingness to shift structural responsibility from an omniscient guiding sense to a submissive withdrawal from both scene and character. The author *creates* both; but he then asks each to communicate for him. What they communicate is on the one hand objective neutrality, on the other finite doubt and uncertainty. The scene is mutely passive; the character is an aesthetic orphan, asked to pay his own way, to narrate at the same time that he exists.

This is what I mean when I say that the philosophical ground of twentieth-century literature has shifted from metaphysics to epistemology. Characters who were formerly maneuvered within an accepted frame of extraliterary reference are now represented as seeking their own definitions and their own languages. This is not to say that metaphysics is abolished; it is always implicit, but the principal course taken by characters is the move toward an awkward and a hesitant initial assumption. They spend much of the time reaching toward a first statement of the first *cogito*. In an extreme example of this change, the opening sentences of Beckett's *The Unnamable* are a revelation of aesthetic finitude: "Where now? Why now? When now? Unquestioning. I, say I. Unbelieving. Questions, hypotheses, call them that. Keep going, going on, call that going, call that on." (*p. 401*)

A world of speculation and introspection has gone into formulating these questions and statements. Characters have assumed and dismissed scores of masks. Moreover, the responsibilities of definition have so long been surrendered to characters that their achievements are limited to the *asking* of questions instead of representing either the full or the partial answers to them. Beckett's "Unnamable" is, as I have said, an extreme case, but he is in his very exaggeration typical. Two important facts belong to our view of him as representative: The first has to do with the author's "disappearance," or more properly to his discreet withdrawal as omniscient personality overtly and conspicuously "in charge" of his creation; the second involves both the reduction and the proliferation of self in modern literature.

This second circumstance has its own ambiguities. From his being a "thinking thing," whose *cogito* confidently anticipates his *sum*, the self has become a groping, stammering, hesitant, fearful thing, a *res haesitans*. Deprived of a priori assurances, he tries to rely upon perceptions of himself as body as a basis of moral decision. But the self as body risks incessantly the dangers of error, corruption, accident. There are no guarantees of purity, continuity, substantiality; there is no guarantor of these. The God of Descartes gave way to the social certainties of Jane Austen and the imagination of Henry James; these were replaced by the diligent imagist or cubist objectivity of Ezra Pound and Gertrude Stein. In these last two cases, the self hid within, or was concealed within, not consciousness itself but imagistic or objective surrogates of the consciousness.

The process of withdrawal continued from there. Time, already reduced to *instants*, becomes space, or a succession or an agglomeration or a confusion of spaces. History becomes a succession of facts (John Dos Passos), with melodramatic highlighting (Frank Norris) or a steady maneuvering of limitation. But even these formal manipulations presume a kind of theoretic control. They were replaced by an even more drastically limited perspective: partly because plots became "thin," partly because the manners of Austen and the conventions of James could no longer be respected, mostly because the creature of the imagination assumed the burden of self-analysis and definition that had earlier been carried by his author. Nathalie Sarraute[2] suggests that the change is also the result of the reader's having acquired an "overbearing sophistication":

> Like the surgeon who eyes the exact spot on which his greatest effort is to be concentrated, isolating it from the rest of the sleeping body, he has been led to center all his attention and curiosity on some new psychological state, forgetting meanwhile the motionless character who serves as a chance prop for this state. He has seen time cease to be the swift stream that carried the plot forward, and become a stagnant pool at the bottom of which a slow, subtle decomposition is in progress; he has seen our actions lose their usual motives and accepted meanings, he has witnessed the appearance of hitherto unknown sentiments and seen those that were most familiar change both in aspect and name.

ii

This chapter has mainly to do with selves and with the relationships of selves to "things." *Things* are in this sense a complex of matter itself, in its several extensions; manners, as these are associated with the human body and the social body involved in exercises of self-determination; and, selves *as* things, or the consciousness of self as body related to objects arranged in the space it occupies. The history of literature, as it affects or is related to a study of Samuel Beckett, is a history of the effort to define self in space and to speculate about its power of initiating and maintaining identity.

Hugh Kenner's brilliant essay, "The Cartesian Centaur," is an indispensable beginning. Kenner depends

for his investigation of Beckett's mechanics upon simple Cartesian principles, those related especially to the
concept of "man as machine" and "man using machine." The basic problem concerns the idea of a perfect machine and the facts of imperfection related to
the human body. If man is a "machine made by the
hands of God," and if the body is in itself a substance
extended in space, how is it that it "defects"? Surely,
it is in itself a most uncertain kind of machine, and
grows more unsteady as its members deteriorate?
Beckett's heroes are engaged in an almost continuous
rational inquiry, which is at one time a testing of the
rational process, at another a check upon the body's
"deserving" as creature the relationship to its creator.
"The Cartesian Centaur is a man riding a bicycle,"
Kenner says, "*mens sana* in *corpore disposito*." [3]

Cartesian relationships are the fundamental necessities of the rational "Enlightenment." They suppose
that the sciences are organically and predictably relevant to each other, to the creation as intrinsic and
perduring schemata; and that they may be reliably
explained by a supervisory science, mathematics.
Geometric figures are the pure outlines of substances,
and in themselves they describe the perfect nature of a
rational universe. Two other facts are necessary to the
comprehension of this design: that matter *extends*
(that it occupies space) and assumes forms, in its extension, that are geometrically describable; second,
that "the essence of the material world is extension
and motion in space." [4] The questions most pertinent
to Beckett's view of the world have to do with the human being as *creature*: Is he in any way responsibly
situated, with respect to other objects, to space independently considered, to the *forms* of matter as it
exists (or is extended) in space; can he consider himself as projected in space if he assumes to himself the

privileged use of other objects (themselves geometrically perfect) and—using them—improves his initial situation; if these objects—in his invention *and* use of them—do enable him to enhance the value of his original properties, can he define himself therefore as an especially endowed creature, communicating with the universal scheme of things; can he therefore establish a relationship to God and be assured that a God may exist with whom a relationship may be established?

Many other questions plague the Beckettian *res cogitans*. May we say that to know God is to assume a God who is capable of creating a thing which knows God? If so, what is the responsible relationship of the God who creates and the creature who knows Him? These are puzzling matters, but the clarity and confidence with which they might be considered involve assumptions accepted in more or less or no faith. They also involve the question of the creator's responsibility for having created a defective creature. Beckett's characters, suspecting or knowing themselves as defective creatures, are deeply suspicious of their creator. Whom are we to blame when the body fails, or when the mind fails to understand it? The Beckett hero scarcely ever conspires to discredit God, but he does discredit and even unwittingly ridicules the elaborate rational machinery designed to explain His ways. The Beckett residual man is a *"fin de partie"* specimen of the breakdown of this machinery. The rational processes become an all but meaningless verbal incantation—like a record moving at the wrong speed or suffering from a stuck needle.

Descartes' speculations put God almost beyond the range of anthropomorphic meditation. The line of progress in rational thought isolated God and generally dismissed the prospects of personal efforts to communicate with Him. Chapter 1 of this book is concerned largely with a type of inquiry (Russian, Jewish) that assumes a close personal commitment of man to God, God to man. However aloof He may at times appear, God is a *personal* issue for Dostoevsky, for his immediate successors, and for Kafka. He is represented in a score of forms, all of them emotionally relevant to the personal status of the inquirer. The line from Descartes to Beckett begins with a separation. Skepticism concerning a universally isolable deity is a *sine qua non* of inquiry. This point of view has the result of making moral speculations a type of convention, an implementation of manners as the form within which self-definition is reached and its behavior measured. The separation of God from man was based briefly and intermittently upon the assumptions that God could be explained rationally, that man could rationally expect His presence, and that he need not "feel" either His presence or agonize over His absence.

The natural consequence of this view was that the validity of self became a matter of his comportment within a narrowly conceived frame. As a rational and skeptical means of speculation, language acquired a value in and of itself. Ambiguities of language provided opportunities for ironic commentary upon the inadequacies of the social animal. Naturally enough, literature stressed consciousness in and of itself, and judged the value of a situation in terms of the ways in which a man reacted to things seen and the quality of his seeing them. Though this is not a literature *of* the Enlightenment, it is a literature that presumes a distance between God and man similar to that accepted in the Enlightenment.

The importance of this view for style and technique cannot be adequately estimated. It has to do with the phenomenon of the author's "disappearing" or defaulting in favor of his characters. It leads to the disposition of overt controls over the work itself. The author converses with his reader, but in no genuine confidence that he will be known or seen as a participant in the conversation. The economy of fiction is a distribution of egos, each of them independently sensitive or eloquent or overcome by uncertainties. Of Descartes one analyst speaks of an inevitable intuition of the "supreme essence": "As the thinking thing, through the anticipatory explorations is led to an ever less inadequate apprehension of the supreme essence, the final fact of inquiry becomes overwhelming in magnitude. It would be inexplicable that the finite thinking thing should achieve these perceptions unless its existence were due to a supreme existent corresponding to the supreme essence." [5] The net result of these "supreme *rapprochements*" of essence and existence is that, unless they are assumed as irreproachable and the self is thereafter portrayed as independently valuable and interesting, no real *literary* self-definition is possible. Metaphysical inquiry all but ceases, or it becomes a kind of moral meditation in terms of social forms and conventions.

The way to "manners" in the novel is made clear. Jane Austen works largely in terms of fixed perceptions, the adequacy of men and women correctly and tastefully to have them, and the irony inherent in emotional or prejudicial extremes. This is not to say that strong feelings were not permitted, but that they were largely self-contained and self-criticized. There is the same general circumstance in the work of both E. M. Forster and Virginia Woolf—this, despite the occasional extravagance of mystic or mythic indulgence. Both are given pause in the necessities of establishing a secular decorum through which the qualities of the self are communicated to its fellows. The *manner* of communication is vastly different in each case: Forster indulges in irony but is reluctant to stare long at vital statistics; Mrs. Woolf is satiric where Forster would be ironic, but she allows her reigning consciousness a metaphysical pathos when she contemplates death and eternity.

The key figure for both is "composition": for Forster, an assumed ideality of human relationship which would "connect the passion and the prose"; for Mrs. Woolf, a "party" arrangement of personalities and minds in "civilized discourse," with underplays and overplays of temperament momentarily suspended:

> There it was, all round them. It partook, she felt, carefully helping Mr. Bankes to a specially tender piece, of eternity; . . . there is a coherence in things, a stability; something, she meant, is immune from change, and shines out (she glanced at the window with its ripple of reflected lights) in the face of the flowing, the fleeting, the spectral, like a ruby; so that again tonight she had the feeling she had had once today, already, of peace, of rest. Of such moments, she thought, the thing is made that endures.[6]

This emphasis upon the self as a center of speculation concerning first and last things, whether presuming and not discussing God or not presuming Him at all, achieves a rich point of sensibility in Henry James. He was not "God-intoxicated" as his father was, but he fully accepted and refined upon the latter's use of the self as a central challenge of human meaning. In a sense, Henry James—like Jane Austen—presumed not God to scan, but only because there was no especial profit in moral speculations with a metaphysical bias. James worked largely in terms of conventions, which were half imagined (that is, invented for the occasion), half based upon the moral and social realities of his time. He was interested in grades of sensitivity, as his characters maneuvered hesitantly from one figuration to another of "what was proper." Each of them needs to define his relationship to other selves and to scenes. Selves complement one another, in the interests of achieving or approaching an ideal fusion of selves. They are above all tested and observed in terms of their reactions to the arrangement of objects in space: masses and unities and ornamental excrescence and tone.

James is writing the novel of the manners of self. God is not absent; he is simply suspended and inactive. The moral convention has taken over. Above all, the validity of a Jamesian self is the object of a venturesome search, an adventure of the self among things. For Lambert Strether, it is the "things" of Woollett, Massachusetts, as against those of Paris; and Strether has a long way to go. Nevertheless, like other James heroes, he *estimates* himself in terms of the tone of his existence within the Parisian space, of the manner in which it stresses by contrast the vulgar naiveté of the spaces he has left. The "assault of images" which inspires Strether to an impassioned sponsorship of "Life," as against the "tin mould . . . into which, a helpless jelly, one's consciousness is poured," [7] is an assault upon his self, toward which he is reaching in an effort to define its scope and specific nature.

The point is that, without the *necessity* of God, or of the metaphysical speculation consequent upon His discernible presence within a society of selves, the novel becomes, first, a novel of manners—that is of understood conventions and an understanding imagination; next, a novel of conscious selves maneuvering through spaces occupied by objects that are either testimonies of or challenges to them; and, finally, of selves almost exclusively, of the "interior selves" of interior monologue. This is a steady development away from metaphysics and toward self-definition *sub specie durationis*.

iii

Language is preserved in this history—if, indeed, it isn't strengthened. It is still an instrument of statement *about* selves; it has moved closer to them, and at times is taken over by them and acquires the color of their current dispositions. The language is *about* something other than universal questions, however, or the universals are assumed as within the particulars of experience. These particulars risk being the sole remnant of consciousness. The record of the consciousness in interior monologue is a record of the ego beginning at least from within. The bias is "from within"; the style assumes the tone of an inner field of perception. The interior monologue allows also for degrees of withdrawal from overt consciousness. In extreme illustrations of the change, the style moves from the first (James, 1881) to the second (Joyce, 1922) of these examples: [8]

> She saw, in the crude light of that revelation which had already become a part of experience and to which the very frailty of the vessel in which it had been offered her only gave an intrinsic price, the dry staring fact that she had been an applied hung-up tool, as senseless and convenient as mere shaped wood and iron.

> The cords of all link back, strandentwining cable of all flesh. That is why mystic monks. Will you be as gods? Gaze in your omphalos. Hello. Kinch here. Put me on to Edenville. Aleph, alpha: nought, nought one.

Joyce's *Ulysses* is almost entirely a novel of textures; not that it does not possess structure, but that it is inferred from the qualities and textures of conscious and interior selves. And, after all, the structure of the novel is on the one hand spatial (that is, the novel is placed within Dublin, and Dublin contains it) and on the other universal by analogy and implication. The universals are held within the particulars; they become universals only if the particulars allow them to be. The quality of the second quotation is an aspect of Stephen Dedalus's tone of mind; it emerges from within Stephen's consciousness and is not derivable in its essentials from the basic presuppositions that originally underplay it. The *quality* of the self is contained within the quality of the language it uses. Further, in Joyce, and in Beckett who follows him, the initial questions raised by the Cartesian dualism, are here revived. We are no longer satisfied with a set of manners or of conventions, nor with the mere texture of skepticism; we see the "supreme essence" of Descartes solely in terms of the fallible existence ("la chose faible") which contemplates it. Here, the style is reduced to the limits of the self (the style *imitates* the self). Subsequently it is to be still further reduced, to resemble not the self but either the objects within spatial approximation of it, or what Nathalie Sarraute calls "sous-conversations": in Sartre's words, "the slow centrifugal creeping of these visions, live solutions." [9]

It amounts to a total secularization of the self, its reduction to the "commonplace." Beckett, writing about *Finnegans Wake* (which was then known only as *Work in Progress*), described Joyce's and Dante's "Purgatory" as significantly contrasting: "Dante's is conical and consequently implies culmination. Mr. Joyce's is spherical and excludes culmination. In the one there is an ascent from real vegetation—Ante-Purgatory, to ideal vegetation—Terrestrial Paradise;

in the other there is no ascent and no ideal vegetation. In the one, absolute progression and a guaranteed consummation: in the other, flux—progression or retrogression, and an apparent consummation." [10]

More significantly, Beckett's favorite image of the *Purgatorio* is that of Belacqua's waiting, like a foetus on a shelf, for the time-span of his human life to release him to Paradise (Canto IV). Beckett's Belacqua (the major character of *More Pricks Than Kicks*, 1934) has no hope of entering Paradise; he does indeed force his experience, choosing both its locale and the companions with whom he is willing to share it. The key word of Beckett's "Joyce" is *vegetation*; Joyce's characters "vegetate," with no prospect of escape from a terrestrial to a Paradisaic level of existence. Their "ascent" is of the sort parodied in Leopold Bloom's escape from an enraged "Citizen," down the streets of Dublin: "And there came a voice out of heaven, calling: *Elijah! Eliajh!* And he answered with a main cry: *Abba! Adonai!* And they beheld Him, ben Bloom Elijah, amid clouds of angels ascend to the glory of the brightness at an angle of forty-five degrees over Donohoe's in Little Green Street like a shot off a shovel." (*p. 339*)

The significance of this passage helps us (perhaps we are too eager to be helped) to further observations concerning Joyce and Beckett. Bloom is not deified, either here or elsewhere; instead, God is Bloomified. The relationship of creator to creature is an absorbing concern in Joyce's works. Once separate the self-defining function from the metaphysical function, and the complications of the relationship become almost intolerably intricate. The Stephen of *A Portrait*, having denied at least the formal institutional requisites of a Creator, becomes in himself a creator; his creatures inhabit his art. But, since the art is itself spun from the thread of his own experience, he is himself the child of his creation. He is also a child of Joyce; and, in the ensuing difficulties of an artist's spinning the subtleties of his life into the fabric of his art, the artist-creation ratio becomes a ratio of artist to creature/artist to creature/artist.

All of these complexities are in themselves set against the disorder and chaos of life. Biology is an adventure in Joyce's fiction: The word *Foetus* carved several times in a student's desk in *Portrait* becomes a symbolic scapegoat in the retreat sermons (not in the sermons themselves, but in the mind of Stephen and in his confession at the end of chapter three); but it is rescued momentarily from the heavy weight of moral and theological condemnation in the vision of a girl at the end of chapter four; ultimately, however, the *Portrait* sets aside the biological processes for the aesthetic. Biology seems to triumph in *Ulysses*: The absence of fertility is lamented (the dead Rudy and the live Stephen are equally inadequate as proofs of virility); gestation and parturition are basic biological realities, and they are approved; masturbation and perversion are themselves contemptible subjects of comedy; and the great Mina Purefoy is the heroine of an episode ("Oxen of the Sun") that frankly celebrates both the sexual act and its fruits: "By heaven, Theodore Purefoy, thou hast done a doughty deed and no botch! Thou art, I vow, the remarkablest progenitor barring none in this chaffering allincluding most farraginous chronicle. Astounding! In her lay a Godframed Godgiven preformed possibility which thou hast fructified with thy modicum of man's work." (416)

We have come a long way from Stephen's revulsion from the word *Foetus* and its suggestion of moral weakness: "It shocked him to find in the outer world a trace of what he had deemed till then a brutish and individual malady of his own mind." [11] But neither in *Ulysses* nor in the *Portrait* is human fertility sentimentally admired; the passage above from *Ulysses* is shot through with ironies. It is for one thing a parody of Carlyle, and the prestigious phrasing is borrowed from him. There are metaphysical echoes in the celebration of biology: as though Mina Purefoy ("la foi pure") were designating her reluctant and wearied spouse as Cartesian instrument. This suggestion is of course dismissed in the novel's context; and Molly's Yes-ing is far too accommodating (and too ingenious) to stand as a positive note in the "farraginous chronicle."

iv

Joyce's sense of the merits of fertility is nevertheless a link with an established life, if not an established literature. The "strandentwining cable of all flesh" that occurs to Stephen (*Ulysses, p.* 39) establishes Joyce as a man committed to basic realities that have supraphysical associations. Surely this commitment is also enforced in *Finnegans Wake*. Beckett's point in the *Exagmination* essay, however, is still pertinent: that Joyce's "Purgatory" is spherical rather than conical. The sphere in this case is self-contained; the body does not rise up to meet its soul, nor the existent to essence.

Beckett is also interested in biological questions, as we shall see. But his characters query the nature and above all the possibility of creation in a spirit of negative distaste. Molloy's speculation about the accident of his creation is relevant: "I know she did all she could not to have me, except of course the one thing, and if she never succeeded in getting me unstuck, it was that fate had earmarked me for less compassionate

sewers." (*Three Novels, p. 19*) It is not only that the
sexual act is rarely if ever praised, or even discussed;
his heroes are both aging and ageless, like the circus
clown, sans teeth, sans everything, who describes his
fate in a few marginal gestures toward infinity and
causality. The movement in Beckett's fiction is toward
impersonal spaces, toward elemental efforts to define
them. The dying animal scarcely knows he has been
alive, and must search for evidence of what "being
alive" means.

It is not that Beckett is preoccupied with anti-life,
nor that he wishes to prove a hateful thesis, like that
of Céline. Rather, as Hugh Kenner says, he returns to
the Cartesian metaphysics and—since metaphysics is
no longer tenable—pursues its implications long after
they have been set aside. He has deliberately mixed
Cartesian geometry with the consequences of two centuries and more of skepticism, to come up with a
mélange of rationality, introspection, brooding over
bodily corruption; he has applied a microscope to the
fungi growing abundantly on the question mark.

The basic symbolic figure of Beckett's work is the
curve, the arc, from the dried up seed of the aging
phallus to the curved lines described in the motion of
a mutilated man with the aid of his crutch. The con-
texts of his novels and plays describe a small space occupied by dimly seen or realized objects, or stretches
of waste spaces whose very monotony offers the very
same impression. In other words, the world is small in
any case, and the imagination is turned uncertainly
inward toward basic introspective doubts. The air is
filled with fascinating but obscure talk, frantic speculations about the logical relationships of trivial objects.

His novels are epistemological inquiries about man-
as-machine and man-using-machine; his plays are re-

sidual reflections upon the existence of God and the imminence of annihilation. Neither theme is precisely indicated; the time is too much taken with the two minimal agonies: over the question whether or not another being exists who (in the fading last rays of the Cartesian sun) may have a meaning for the self; over the terrible necessity to "wait." As we shall see in Chapters 4 and 5, the romantically rich despair of Baudelairian ennui is now reduced to a dehydrated and de-animated "waiting."

In *L'Ère du soupçon*, Nathalie Sarraute speaks of Dostoevsky's having "opened the way" to the examination of a world which Kafka has followed "jusqu'au bout." The underground man is the beginning of an analysis which reaches its conclusion in Beckett and his French contemporaries. But I think also that there are important differences. While they share a distrust of logicality, Dostoevsky's man differs from Beckett's "I" and the anti-heroes of contemporary French drama and fiction in their dispositions toward both logic and fact. Freed of his ironic and speculative "master," Dostoevsky's undergroundling might have behaved in a manner similar to one of Beckett's "M's" or Miss Sarraute's "homme inconnu." It is true that since the *Notes from the Underground* familiar landmarks of human relationship are less in evidence; but major attitudes have changed, from the temperamental establishment of the ego to a limited appraisal of the ego's position in a world of others, spatially related and measured.

Perhaps the major stresses are upon *things* and upon language. The novels and plays of Beckett's contemporaries lack direct ideological controls or focus. In some cases they are direct attacks upon ideologies of which their authors have been disabused, or attacks upon discredited language practices and conventions.

In any case, the result is a reduction in scope and valuation of the meaning of language and things. J. Robert Loy has usefully summarized this shift in perspective: [12]

> Thus we are not concerned here with the historical and descriptive background of the Romantics (Hugo's sewers in *Les Misérables*), or with the documentary display of wares in the Naturalists (Zola's meats and vegetables in *Le Ventre de Paris*), or the long studies of things which are, in another way, so important a part of Proust's world. We are, metaphysically and stylistically, worlds away from the special objective-subjective vision of Flaubert. . . . To the exclusion of persons and ideas, the inanimate object becomes the literary subject; it is the persons, if any, the ideas and the emotions that form the descriptive background, if and when it exists.

The implications offer a fascinating look at recent literature: for Dostoevsky's underground man, things either mirror the self or testify to its primary situation; as for Sartre's Roquentin and Camus' Meursault, their experiences with things overwhelm them with a realization of "the absurd"; in many of the situations described in Robbe-Grillet's fiction, things and spaces are the only reliable descriptive marks of the narrative situation. All of these variants have a relevance to Beckett's use of things. Superficially, objects in his novels and plays appear to be useful supports or a means of maneuvering. They turn out to be basic elements of philosophical inquiry: their value as extensions of the bodies of his M's is diligently tested; their geometrical natures are scrupulously defined; and, in combinations or sequences, they are restlessly explored, catalogued, analyzed. The *quidditas* of Stephen Dedalus's aesthetic becomes the Watt of Beckett's novel as Stephen's *non serviam* gesture becomes the burdensome question of Watt's service to Knott.

Persons as traditionally viewed frequently disappear, or if they exist they are scapegoats of an elaborate epistemological vaudeville "routine." Eugène Ionesco's plays are often elaborate spoofs; the pretensions of stability, virtue, progress are echoed, repeated, played upon and exaggerated.[13] The climax of *The Chairs* is typical. The Old Man and his wife have gathered many friends and celebrities (they are visible only as chairs) for an impressive ceremony; he has hired an "Orator" to make a significant statement: [14]

OM   We will leave some traces, for we are people and not cities.

OM   and OW [*together*]   We will have a street named after us.

OM   Let us be united in time and in eternity, even if we are not together in space, as we were in adversity: let us die at the same moment . . . [*To the Orator, who is impassive, immobile:*] One last time. . . . I place my trust in you . . . I count on you. You will tell all . . . bequeath my message . . .

The Orator is discovered to be deaf and dumb, and can only offer the guttural sounds of a mute: "He, mme, mm, mm. Ju, gon, hou, hou. Heu, heu, gu gou, gueue." Finally he writes a few letters on the blackboard: "ANGELFOOD," then: "NNAA NNM NWNWNW V," and finally: "ΛΛADIEU ΛDIEU ΛPΛ."

There is a difference between technique and aim in these works. Ionesco is largely concerned to use his "cross-purposes" theatre in prolonged satires of bourgeois circumstance and emptiness; on other occasions (*Amédée, The Killer*), he directly parodies the conventions of "progress." Alain Robbe-Grillet is less overtly ambitious. He relies upon things and spaces as substances or realities; they direct the reader's attention to persons (that is, persons exist in relation to things), but they are not supposed to stimulate emotions or call up stock responses.

> At every instant, a continuous fringe of culture (psychology, ethics, metaphysics, etc.) is being added to things, disguising their real strangeness, making them more comprehensible, more reassuring. . . .
>
> But the world is neither significant nor absurd. It *is*, quite simply. That, in any case, is the most remarkable thing about it. And suddenly this evidence strikes us with irresistible force. All at once the whole beautiful construction collapses: opening our eyes to the unexpected, we have experienced once too often the shock of this stubborn reality we were pretending to have mastered. Around us, defying the mob of our animistic or protective adjectives, the things *are there*.[15]

The range of techniques is significant. Robbe-Grillet presents the ordinary narrative with the plot removed —or at best, to be inferred. Jean Genet's plays come at moral issues from the "wrong end"; what is conventionally alleged to be evil, wicked, or illegal, is transformed, to become the norm. He is, in Sartre's words, a saint "en vermine." [16] But, while Dostoevsky's anti-hero disgustedly compares himself to an insect and Kafka's Gregor Samsa endures the terrors of his metamorphosis, Genet assumes his as a normal beginning. The "worst" is not necessarily "the best," but it is a proper point of departure for viewing life. The net result is that conventional life is seen from the other end of the telescope. For Genet, terror and evil have their properties, and a representation of life along these lines must assume them as a minimum. The consequences are like those of Ionesco's, but the techniques are radically different. In either case, playgoers are rudely shocked out of conventional expectations—as indeed they are at performances of Beckett's plays. Martin Esslin has put the matter simply: [17]

The Theatre of the Absurd shows the world as an incomprehensible place. The spectators see the happenings on the stage entirely from the outside, without ever understanding the full meaning of these strange patterns of events, as newly arrived visitors might watch life in a country of which they have not yet mastered the language. . . . Emotional identification with the characters is replaced by a puzzled, critical attention. For while the happenings on the stage are absurd, they yet remain recognizable as somehow related to real life with *its* absurdity, so that eventually the spectators are brought face to face with the irrational side of their existence.

v

The "irrational side" of human existence is only one phase of this literature. All of it has common values and employs variants of a single technique; but the infinite variety of this literature demands some effort to sum it up: One may rationally probe irrationality, or offer a pure irrationality; one may use objects as the central focus of a narrative or as extensions of the self as matter existing in space; one may concentrate upon sub-rational substances underlying the disguises of "inauthentic behavior" (what Miss Sarraute calls "sous-conversation"); one may treat disorder as order, or as preferable to order, or may point to conventional order as incredibly tedious and patently deceitful. Attitudes and techniques are in all these cases closely associated. Invariably, things are "not what they seem": they are designed not to be. Styles and techniques are bound to be confusing and shocking. The reader or audience puzzles through the performance, struggling to stay at some center, fearful of going "way out" and getting lost, finally resigned to the technical necessities of the absurd.

It is not entirely because this is an "absurd world."

The absurdity is an essential characteristic, surely. But the "obscurities" are caused as much by the fact that the characters in this literature are "logical" beings as by the fact of their existing in an absurd world. It is a matter of the shift from a metaphysical ground to an epistemological search for new certainties. The emphasis has changed from a world of universal presuppositions to an assortment of selves without them. It is a bit like the act of appointing a committee to examine the validity of the act of appointing committees. The language of the act in any case is not dissimilar from that of any other act, but it doesn't "*mean* the same things it used to mean."

One needs to stress again and again the roles of logic, rationality, the proprieties of arrangements, in this literature. In fact, the *strength* of the rational mind is a primary cause of obscurity. Let me try to summarize the forces leading to this situation. We begin with Cartesian certainties, which depend fundamentally upon a power of mathematical description of certitudes and a willingness to forego skepticism concerning God's role in the management of the universal machine. From this point, rationality "takes over"; that is, a reasonable world is assumed, and literature fixes its attention upon manners, with a range of useful ironies which act as a check upon human absurdities. There is a change, however, from *je pense* to *je me doute* as the essential beginning of meditation. The focus changes from a level of assumed manners to one of uncertain selves. At first, these uncertainties are only relative to the strength of original confidences from which they have declined. But, gradually and steadily, the fact of inquiry merges with the nature of the inquirer.

The fact that doubt has become a central means of speculation does not rule out the utility of logic or rational language practices. It simply means that both will decline from a position of linguistic certainty to one of increasingly erratic usage. The orderly processes disappear by which defined particulars may invariably and accurately illustrate self-evident laws or principles—leaving a language that is useful to them, but encourages chaos in any other context. We approach the reign of Ubu Roi. The social scene is radically transposed; the rational conventions are clichés or comic and pathetic sentimentalities.

Tests of existence also radically change. The self finds the proof of existence exasperatingly difficult or a painful responsibility. Correspondingly, those selves who are not sensitive to the challenge of existence are presented as ludicrous; they are in the world of the absurd as such, but they are a part of it without being aware of themselves, and they therefore increase and perpetuate its absurdity. There are degrees and shades of awareness between the two extremes.

The basic materials of Beckett's work are selves as inquiring beings, selves as objects, other objects, and the degrees and forms of distance between one of these and another. There are no clear lines of differentiation: Both inanimate objects and distances have universal properties, or rather residual properties left over from the Cartesian universe. Beckett's heroes describe lines and curves of relationship. They are first of all disturbed over the matter of creation (cannot determine if they or a "something other" is a creator); secondly are puzzled over the question of the identity of created things (if the original creative source is not clearly known, it follows that creatures will be confused with one another); finally are engaged in the bewildering process of defining objects, as individually and separately objects or as extensions of the self.

All of these facts about Beckett's world set it off

from that of his contemporaries. Both illogicality and absurdity have already been assumed; Beckett is not concerned to prove either one. Instead, his writings are attenuations of meaning: a ceaseless and noisy and repetitious echoing of logical questions and near-definitions. Robbe-Grillet is forever about the business of avoiding fake emotional inferences from the world of existence. Ionesco exploits surface absurdities, invests them with elaborate schemes of overt ambiguity. Nathalie Sarraute plays a game of hidden motives, so that the presumed reasons for acting and talking are all but drowned in the real ones.

These arc distinct qualities, and their peculiarities join to give contemporary literature a wide range of "absurd" representations. But they also argue quite separate dispositions to the problems of self-definition. Beckett's emerges from the world of Joyce, whom he had served in one capacity or another (translator, reader, critic) during the period of "Work in Progress." It is both a development from Joyce and distinctly different. The terms are similar: both are disposed to examine universals within secular limits; both exploit the comical-pathetic in commonplace experience; both arc master analysts of the relations of words to being. But Beckett is far less interested in erudition as a value in itself, or fond of playing out the sounds and values of words to the end of their literary usefulness. Beckett's narrating ego, though he may be ludicrously unsure of himself from beginning to end, is entirely "in charge of" what he says; he is never an "example" of his author's skill and ingenuity in providing him with ways of saying it.

BEYOND MEMORY:
PERSPECTIVES IN MODERN
LITERATURE

"THERE IS NO ESCAPE from the hours and the days,"
Beckett says in his essay on *Proust*. "Neither from to-
morrow nor from yesterday." (*p. 2*) The essay is the
most significant of all Beckett's critical statements,
far more revealing of what he was yet to write than of
what Proust had written. In a seventy-two page essay,
written this time in English, Beckett explored the
problems of habit and its opposite, spontaneity; of the
separate parts of the individual ego; of time and of
death.

I should like to consider this essay, not as an example of Beckett as critic (he is not significantly an
analyst of other men's works) but as a prolegomenon
to the novels and plays to come. Proust offered a useful point of departure, though Beckett was not significantly influenced by him. Basically, the Proustian
struggle to rescue and preserve the self from time was
Beckett's cue. For him as for Proust, the self fought
steadily to avoid immersion in nonentity, to assert
identity. Beckett therefore appreciates the Proustian
goal as the sustenance of the ego, keeping it above the
flux of ordinary time and enclosing it within vital
cages of memory. "The individual is the seat of a
constant process of decantation, decantation from the
vessel containing the fluid of future time, sluggish,

pale and monochrome, to the vessel containing the fluid of past time, agitated and multicoloured by the phenomena of the hours." (4–5)

The self is many selves, and the problem is to assert a continuous self-identity. In habit this identity is maintained at the expense of distinction. Beckett defines habit as "the generic term for the countless treaties concluded between the countless subjects that constitute the individual and their countless correlative objects" (8). This statement admirably defines the condition of the Beckett hero, who strives loudly and desperately to "count himself in" as a self; he undergoes elaborate routines of repetition, draws up fantastically intricate charts of possibilities inherent in habitual decision and action. The genuine *crisis* of being occurs in the transition from one phase of habitual being to another: "The periods of transition that separate consecutive adaptations (because by no expedient of macabre transubstantiation can the gravesheets serve as swaddling clothes) represent the perilous zones in the life of the individual, dangerous, precarious, painful, mysterious and fertile, when for a moment the boredom of living is replaced by the suffering of being." (8)

Presumably this "adventure of being" becomes, in Beckett's later work, the occasion for specific identification of self; though habit is also a difficult resource of being for the Beckett hero. Security of self is in all respects difficult to maintain, and on many occasions the act of "waiting" is an heroic function. Waiting involves not only watching for a sign of being (a repetition of something remembered, a movement in gestures that have a recognizable line or curve). The true heroics of the self come in such moments of crisis when its acts do not assure or guarantee a continuous identity: "The mortal microcosm cannot forgive the relative immortality of the macrocosm" (10). As is the case of À *la recherche du temps perdu* (though in an entirely different context), the Beckett ego strives constantly to match his "microcosmic self" (if he can be sure of that) against any universal structure of being it suggests or he can remember or devise.

The ego then must rescue itself from oblivion, as Proust's hero finds it necessary each morning to "resume consciousness" at the risk of not finding the self he was the day before. Proust's adventure is contained largely in memory; present sensation may release a flow of past sensations which will secure the self. These are almost always sensations: tastes, touches, the grain of an object's surface in contact with the texture of the flesh, sounds, even sentiments. They are the *qualities* of objects, but they are not regarded as intrinsically objects. Beckett's adventures of self were to be concerned more exactly with objects. He is different from Proust, as Descartes is from Bergson. The challenge is not so much to memory as it is to reason; the Beckett hero is engaged in ceaseless "rational" speculation concerning the questions of who, what, where am I. "But when the object is perceived as particular and unique and not merely the member of a family, when it appears independent of any general notion and detached from the sanity of a cause, isolated and inexplicable in the light of ignorance, then and then only may it be a source of enchantment." (11)

This is the precise ratio used by Beckett's characters: not only the exact identity of the object, but its role in extending the self, its attachment to it, resemblance to it, or distance from it. Objective relationships are consistently a challenge. So, the boot and the hat in *Waiting for Godot*, the stick in *Malone Dies*, the earthen pot in *The Unnamable*, the bicycle in

Molloy and other places: these are both extensions of bodies and guarantors of identity. As the body's members lose their strength, or are shortened, or disappear altogether, the task of precisely maintaining the self within macrocosmic lines and curves becomes more and more difficult; until the ultimate powers of creation (*Malone Dies, The Unnamable*) or destruction (*Endgame*) are brought in to effect a final rescue of the self.

Beckett points to the terror Proust's hero feels before the movement of time, "the perpetual exfoliation of personality" (13) and the change of one individual into many variant aspects of itself, finally the threat of indifference which succeeds to the loss of consciousness of personal relationships. Proust's Marcel therefore needs a grasp of permanence in the flux, fastens upon enduring images that recur from the memory and formally endure "au cadre du temps." Beckett's own characters suffer from a similar terror, though their acts consist primarily in the adventure of motion away from a fixed point. Even Malone thinks what he could do if the bed on which he is dying had casters: He might have moved into and even out of the room. But the motion has geometrical unities, as Proust's has aesthetic. Molloy moves toward Moran, Moran toward Molloy, until the two are composed as one creation. When motion is impossible, the self has recourse to static extensions of body, the space thus encompassed enlarging. Malone's stick enables him to exist, as his pencil is the means of creative extension; both are the surrogates of his sexual powers, which have been "hurt" by age and disease. In every case, the fear of annihilation in Beckett's men is the result of physical deprivation; they are heroes in persisting in spite of it and beyond it: in manipulating a crutch around the world's curvature, inching ahead in a ditch

into which they have fallen; failing all powers of motion, they at least search for evidences that they are
still selves. The motion diminishes, from the bicycle
to the crutch to the stick to the wheel chair to the bed.
All of this occurs within space, while Proust's hero rescues himself within the memory and imagination.

Beckett marvels over the transformations of self in
À la recherche. The many selves of Marcel's memory
of Albertine persist beyond the fact of her death:
"Her death, her emancipation from time, does not
calm his jealousy nor accelerate the extinction of an
obsession whose rack and wheel were the days and
the hours" (43). Other characters undergo similar
changes of identity. But the self is rescued only in the
memory of other selves, and the sole means of rescue
is Love. "We are alone. We cannot know and we cannot be known. 'Man is the creature that cannot come
forth from himself, who knows others only in himself, and who, if he asserts the contrary, lies.'" (49)

In Proust's case, the self creates and sustains images
of others in its memory, finally consolidates these as
objects of memory, whose texture conquers time. Both
Proust and Beckett take over the God-like function of
creativity. Eternity is not assumed, and God does not
appear; the creative efforts of Proust's and Beckett's
heroes are improvisational. Creativity is strongest near
the moment of death; the pencil of Malone does what
the phallus of Macmann cannot do. Proust's hero re-
stricts himself to the task of solidifying memory;
Beckett's men go beyond, to create themselves and
their several variants. Their bodies occupy space; but
bodies are projections of mind, a rudimentary parthe-
nogenesis. To cause themselves is a guarantee as
strong as any other of their being. It is a form of ego-
persistence, in the prospect of diminishing physical
powers. We must create one another or die.

Beckett's admiration of Proust is well deserved, but they are nevertheless far apart in their philosophical assumptions. In 1930, Beckett published a poem, *Whoroscope,* an avowed imitation of Eliot and Joyce; it exists primarily because he had entered a contest for poems about Time, and it was published because it won the contest. The poem anticipates his basic interests in Descartes, who is its protagonist. It is much involved in the kind of dream elaboration that Joyce was developing in what was to be *Finnegans Wake.* It is concerned with the generation of life (the egg) and the function of the intellect (the syllogism). Beckett here contemplates in absolute disdain the depravities of the body which cannot hope for much of the guarantee Descartes had offered it of immortality. Eating the egg, drinking the wine, the body goes through a mock ceremony of creation and immortality, each of them and self-continuance as well having been guaranteed in the Cartesian universe.

The metaphor of The Incarnation has short shrift:

> *So we drink Him and eat Him*
> *and the watery Beaune and the stale cubes of Hovis*
> *because He can jig*
> *as near or as far from His jigging Self*
> *and as sad or lively as the chalice or the tray asks.*[1]

This rejection of the sacrament is a satire of Descartes' discomfort when he was obliged to accommodate his theory to the fact of the Eucharist. Similarly, God is assumed not proved; or if proved proved "by exhaustion," as Beckett puts it in his notes to lines 77–83. What is left is the man Descartes eating his omelette ("made of eggs hatched from eight to ten days") and fumbling over the necessities and failures forced by the omission of human assurances from his philosophy. These failures were to be acted out and deliberated in countless ways in the work to come. Not the least of these is the way of the comic, the clown, the hobo who waits for Godot, or who reaches eagerly though unavailingly for a hand, a rope, a tree that are offered then pulled away from him. ("Acts Without Words: I")

ii

For Beckett, the clown's gestures are a way of appealing, solemnly but also wryly, to metaphysical certainties that in their very nature are guaranteed not to exist; or, assuming their nonexistence at the start, they are comic forms of intellectual concentration. Hugh Kenner [2] likens them to Emmett Kelly's "solemn determination to sweep a circle of light into a dustpan: a haunted man whose fidelity to an impossible task—quite as if someone he desires to oblige had exacted it of him—illuminates the dynamics of a tragic sense of duty."

The task is "impossible"; had it been achieved, it would have been meaningless; the gestures and the decorum of the actor are ludicrous. All of these facts are true; yet the performance itself has a melancholy dignity. It is the performance of a man striving to be more than an existent being, sometimes indeed to maintain the minimum characteristics of existence itself. Emmett Kelly's gesture is both comic and dignified because it points to an unachievable universal power. The greatest comedy in Beckett and his contemporaries is found in the paradoxes of infinity-finitude, and of order-disorder. Bérenger of Ionesco's *The Killer* represents the second. Frantically pursuing the criminal—who is himself a comic extension of evil—he encounters an incredible tangle of traffic, directed arbitrarily by two policemen. They aren't in the slightest bit interested in a criminal-at-large, but concentrate on the problem of orderly traffic. Bérenger, anxious to solve the larger problem of order, merely obstructs the smaller.

BÉRENGER   The criminal must pay for his crime!
1ST POL.   Phew! They can talk themselves silly, some of them!
2ND POL.   [*louder, turning to Bérenger again*] It's not my racket, get it? I don't give a good goddam for your story. If you're one of the boss's pals, go and see him and leave me in goddam peace. [3]

In many examples of gestural comedy, minor skills and graces become the equivalent—for children and other unspoiled humans—of infinite powers; as in Richard Wilbur's poem, "Juggler," [4] where the performer becomes magus, extending his skills beyond the simple objects and the limited curves of motion through which he guides them.

It takes a sky-blue juggler with five red balls

To shake our gravity up. Whee, in the air
The balls roll round, wheel on his wheeling hands,
Learning the ways of lightness, alter to spheres
Grazing his finger ends,
Cling to their courses there,
Swinging a small heaven about his ears.

In the great tradition of nineteenth-century French poetry, the clown is a man reduced to comical-pathetic extremes: the "guignon," the "pitre," the "chiffonnier," are not so often clowns as specimens of reduced humanity, whose powers of self-extension have diminished almost to the vanishing point; but in the deterioration, they achieve a dignity withheld from the bourgeoisie, whose motions are simply ludicrous and tedious. The formalized clown—the Harlequin, the Pierrot—combines his pitifulness with the standards of high passion and thought from which it is a degeneration. Laforgue's clown is the Hamlet *presque manqué*, stylized and literate, though none the less a reduction of universals.

> *Upon a white and starchèd ruff,*
> *A neck that's equally as stiff,*
> *Rests a hairless, cold-creamed face*
> *Like hydrocephalic asparagus.*
>
> *The eyes are drowned in the opium*
> *Of universal self-indulgence;*
> *The harlequin mouth casts a spell*
> *Like a singular geranium.*
>
> *A mouth which alternates the while*
> *Between a glacial, uncorked O,*
> *And the transcendental overflow*
> *Of the proud Gioconda smile.*[5]

The stylization of the clown is a step away from pathos, toward sophistication. Laforgue ridicules universals by playing upon their terminologies and by investing his Pierrots with a fashionable irony. They can be taken seriously, but they do not strongly "relate" to the universal world of which they are so obvious a reduction. The meaningful clown, of the meaningful gesture, is associated with the heavens and the earth to which he is, in a certainty of failure, concerned significantly to relate. He describes the spheres, and imitates them; his mind and spirit both stagger across the tightrope; he wishes to establish a *rapport* of his rhythms with what he thinks are universal rhythms. Laforgue's clowns are inept and ludicrous; but their failings are commentaries on pompous metaphysical generalities. The significance of the line of descent from Baudelaire's chiffonniers to Beckett's "bums" is that their reaction to experience is not just an ironic commentary upon it, but an actual participation in it. The effort to "sweep a circle of light into a dustpan" is at least akin to the juggler's and the acrobat's emulation of the rhythms and lines of the starry heavens and of the earth in its course. It is in the very nature of these attempts that they should fail; both the comedy and the pathos depend upon the failure.

While Laforgue's Pierrots suggest or appeal to wit and sophistication, the antics of circus clowns, of vaudeville and burlesque actors, of Charlie Chaplin and Buster Keaton, appeal to fundamental instincts. They aspire to what we also wish to do, and their failure is a shared failure. Robert Payne [6] describes Chaplin as a descendant of the great god Pan, who first appeared on the modern scene in February of 1914:

> He came jauntily, swinging his cane, wearing a seedy cutaway, a dilapidated derby hat, enormous out-turned boots, baggy pants and an absurd toothbrush mustache. As for the cane, it was all that was left to him of the goatherd's flowering staff. Head erect, pale from exhaustion, with livid black rings round his eyes, his mouth twitching, he came down a street in Venice, California, as though he owned the place, and if he was hungry and down-at-heel, it was observed that there was something of the prince about him.

Chaplin's gestures—the shrug of the shoulders, twitch of the mustache, the bowlegged walk, the mixture of "sincerity" and sentimentality, above all the survival of incalculable dangers, are all of them imitations of a human nature free of pretension and profundity. So too, the deadpan earnestness of Buster Keaton, who can make a shambles of a love affair or a Beethoven sonata, remains within the curve of the commonplace buffoon. These characteristic motions

are akin to the grosser gestures of the music hall and
burlesque houses. Staying well this side of sentimental
romanticism, burlesque clowns attempt feats of im-
probable virility, or move ungracefully to the archetypal pratfall, or describe infinite extensions of the
phallus presiding over an infinitely accommodating
womb. Perhaps their ultimate expression is the cyclist who describes repetitive though erratic circles
about the stage, while he keeps a half dozen balls or
oranges circling in the air and chatters obscenities to
the audience. This is the composite clown, acrobat,
juggler and burlesque comic; he is the extreme reduction of the Cartesian "matter in motion," entirely
secularized and reduced to the level of the arduous
gesture with no meaning.

The importance of this kind of art lies in its containing universals within abject particulars. The in-
spiration and the skill come "from within." They have
a close relationship to the achievements of Beckett's
"bums," except that these latter both act out and talk
out improbabilities. The rationalist logorrhea of Beckett's heroes is a version of the physical repetitions of
burlesque house jokes. Both are a matter of filling in
the spaces of "waiting," whether for Godot or for the
next train and rooming house doesn't matter. They are
both comically earnest, and marked by similar
stretches of boredom and stylized action. Neither assumes a divine purpose guiding the act or the waiting;
the responsibility for the quality of gesture is in each
case a *raison d'être*. Each says in effect: this is the
way I interpret the universe, or God's will, or human
passions and imperfections. Each exists independently
of purpose; the act itself defines the meaning thereof.
Above all, the actions and the talk are isolated and are
expressions of the supreme fact of isolation. In every
case, the actor-talker is defective, not whole or proper

or tidy or distinguished. He operates from his imperfection to aesthetic exploitation of it, or of its meaning as a sign of an imperfection in a patchwork universe.

Beckett's *Textes pour rien* present these gestures in an almost pure and plotless talk, the final result of what Kenner in his *Spectrum* article calls "immaculate solipsism compelled . . . to talk, talk, talk, and fertile in despairing explanations for its own garrulity." Here, in this final expression of the disembodied voice, the uncertainties and indefinitudes become a comic routine: "Suddenly, no, at last, long last, I couldn't any more, couldn't go on. Someone said, You can't stay there. I couldn't stay there and I couldn't go on. I'll describe the place, that's unimportant. The top, very flat, of a mountain, no, a hill, but so wild, so wild, enough." [7] There are echoes of people and places, but the texts are all but literally "pour rien"; not *from* nothing but *for* the state of nothingness. The "I" creates himself, or doesn't want to be created, and struggles against his creation by himself. The intonations and involutions of the style are a Beckettian version of "patter": not jokes, not obscenities, but almost pure garrulousness.

If it is hard to see these texts as a culmination of the clown's or the comedian's art, it may be well to remember that they are an extension of *Watt* and the trilogy. They are the ultimate expression in words without acts of what Beckett's pantomimes are in "Acts Without Words I." [8]

Desert, Dazzling light.
The man is flung backwards on stage from right wing.
He falls, gets up immediately, dusts himself, turns aside, reflects.

Beside carafe a rope descends from flies, with knots to facilitate ascent.

He turns, sees rope, reflects, goes to it, climbs up it and is about to reach carafe when rope is let out and deposits him back on ground.

iii

Peggy Guggenheim, who met him in Paris late in 1937, called Beckett her "Oblomov"; [9] she had in mind perhaps the notion of an intellectual of irregular habits and an indisposition to change himself or accommodate to others.

Oblomov was a tall lanky Irishman of about thirty with enormous green eyes that never looked at you. He wore spcctacles, and always seemed to be far away solving some intellectual problem; he spoke very seldom and never said anything stupid. He was excessively polite, but rather awkward. He dressed badly in tight-fitting French clothes and had no vanity about his appearance. Oblomov accepted life fatalistically, as he never seemed to think he could alter anything. He was a frustrated writer, a pure intellectual.

It is hard to see how she could have given him the nickname, unless she had read Dobrolyubov's essay instead of Goncharov's novel.[10] Miss Guggenheim's memoir is almost pure gossip, though she is vaguely correct in her estimate of Joyce's influence and of its limits: Beckett "did have certain strange and morbid ideas which were quite original and a wonderfully sardonic sense of humor."

By 1937, Beckett had published two short sequences of poems, a volume of short stories, and two critical essays. Three facts emerge concerning the man at the edge of his major career (*Murphy* was published in 1938): he had spent most of his time appreciating and imitating his "elders" (Joyce, Eliot, Proust); he had explored Dante's Hell and the ante-Purgatory (he was not to go far beyond the latter); and he had already indicated the direction his original work might go. That "he always seemed to be far away solving some intellectual problem" is already testified to in his relationships to Joyce, in the kinds of "nominalistic discourse" he engaged in with him,[11] and in the critical position he so obviously took in the Joyce and Proust essays.

In his "exagmination" of Joyce (*p. 22*), Beckett speaks of Joyce's "Work in Progress" as "purgatorial" and defines the term in this way: "Hell is the static lifelessness of unrelieved viciousness. Paradise the static lifelessness of unrelieved immaculation. Purgatory a flood of movement and vitality released by the conjunction of these two elements." The world is dominated by the "partially purged," whose moral values result from the tension between hellish and paradisaic extremes. Beckett's major work was to be confined to the purgatorial locale, a place which offered endless opportunities for human reflection and measurement at the very time when both the kind and the duration of human inadequacies were being endured and examined.

In the Hell of "unrelieved viciousness," there was little or no room for moral movement, no occasion for profitable reflection, only a looking back at the causes of fixed and irrevocable punishments. In modern literature, however, there is scarcely ever an occasion that entirely escapes the Inferno: for Eliot the streets of his London and Baudelaire's Paris, for Joyce the graphic descriptions of physical and spiritual pain extended (*Portrait*) and the Nighttown scene of *Ulysses*. Beckett also has his *Inferno*. It is like Joyce's in certain language values, like Eliot's in its span of several European cities. *Echo's Bones* (1932) is a journey through this kind of hell. It is smart and "up-to-date" and imitative; and it is haunted by the vision of irrevocable mortality:

> *asylum under my tread all this day*
> *their muffled revels as the flesh falls*
> *breaking without fear or favour wind*
> *the gantelope of sense and nonsense run*
> *taken by the maggots for what they are* [12]

The protagonist of *Echo's Bones* (apparently Miss Guggenheim's "Oblomov") travels through a world whose "atmosphere is fetid and unsustained"; [13] his observations are charged by a melancholy sense of ominous certitude. In Dublin, he leaves the Portobello Nursing Home:

> *my skull sullenly*
> *clot of anger*
> *skewered aloft strangled in the cang of the wind*
> *bites like a dog against its chastisement.* (*p.* 179)

A "little wearish old man" combines the qualities of Baudelaire's *vieillards* and Beckett's Molloy, *et al.*:

> *scuttling along between a crutch and a stick,*
> *his stump caught up horribly, like a claw,*
> > *under his breech,*
> *smoking.* (*p.* 180)

Young men, "a great perturbation of sweaty heroes,/ in their Sunday best,/come hastening for a pint of nepenthe or moly/or half and half" (*p.* 181). These are offered in the spirit of Dante's and Eliot's ante-Hell, the equivalent at the moment at least of fixed mortality: "de morituris nihil nisi" (*p.* 182). The lines that follow strongly echo Eliot's of *Ash Wednesday*, Part Three, but are also obviously a parody of them.

The desire to return to the womb, to avoid the hellishness of existence, alternates with a wish to hurry toward the grave:

> ah to be back in the caul now with no trusts
> no fingers no spoilt love
> belting along in the meantime clutching the bike
> the billows of the nubile the cere wrack
> pot-valiant caulless waisted in rags hatless
> for mamma papa chicken and ham
> warm Grave too say the word (p. 183)

These lines are followed by the suggestion of a frantic search through literature for answers, but the "main verb at last" is achieved, to copulate:

> her whom alone in the accusative
> I have dismounted to love (p. 184)

The scene changes, from Dublin to Paris, where the "slouching happy body/loose in my stinking old suit" pauses at the American Bar, in rue Mouffetard (p. 185); from there to London, the "grand old British Museum" and Regent's Park:

> I find me taking the Crystal Palace
> for the Blessed Isles from Primrose Hill (p. 187)

In both cities he is the bum anticipating death, meditating upon frail mortality:

> my brother the fly
> the common housefly
>
> sidling out of darkness into light
> fastens on his place in the sun
> whets his six legs
> revels in his planes his poisers
> it is the autumn of his life
> he could not serve typhoid and mammon (p. 188)

Throughout, the poems are dominated by this sense of the useless body and certain death. It is an observer's world, to which the mind is alert but the passion uncommitted. The general impression is that of a camera eye ("all these phantoms shuddering out of focus"); there is little but the most elementary and amateurish reaction to what is seen. The cleverness and the erudition are both borrowed and unformed. *Echo's Bones* helps to define Beckett's early place in literature; he is too close to contemporary masters, too much in their shadow, to speak his mind independently of them. The work is valuable only as a means of identifying his relationship to them and of anticipating special preoccupations that will take over from them. The fact that both *Finnegans Wake* and *Murphy* appeared in 1938 may have some significance, as a suggestion that Beckett was to go "on his own," once the blinding genius of the master had achieved its final form.

iv

The hero of Beckett's volume of short stories, *More Pricks Than Kicks* (1934) is called Belacqua Shuah. The figure of Belacqua appears in Dante's ante-Purgatory (*Purgatorio*, Canto IV); in One, Dante and Vergil wander along "that lonely plain" where the souls wait who have not yet entered Purgatory, lost to the world and not ready for their stay in Purgatory. They are sure of nothing, neither of the character of their recent departure from earth nor of what they may soon expect. It is a state of blankness and indecision, and it may thus be assumed a symbolic parallel of the conditions of many earthly souls. As Francis Fergusson has put it,[14] "They still have the potentialities of sane growth, if they could only discover how to begin. Their plight is thus like that of the human creature in general when deprived of a living tradition; or like that of every child or young

person who has not yet found himself in his world."
Belacqua is one of those who, from indolence, delayed
repentance until their last hour; they are therefore
punished by a delay in entering the Purgatory, for a
period equal in length to their lives.

In Canto IV, lines 106–135, Dante discusses Belacqua's plight with him. He sits upon a massive
boulder, his hands clasping his knees, "Only his face
upon his thigh," assuming therefore a foetal position
apparently for the equivalent of his lifetime.

> "Brother," said he, "What use to go up yet?
> He'd not admit me to the cleansing pain,
> That bird of God who perches at the gate.
>
> My lifetime long tho heavens must wheel again
> Round me, that to my parting hour put off
> My healing sighs; and I meanwhile remain
>
> Outside, unless prayer hasten my remove—
> Prayer from a heart in grace; for who sets store
> By other kinds, which are not heard above?" [15]

The situation here described is not unlike that suffered by Beckett's own characters—except that, as
Walter Strauss says,[16] they "do not even have that
much certitude about their spiritual destination, and
thus are left in a state of complete disorientation."
Strauss continues, calling Beckett "the poet of vegetation," a term Beckett had himself used in his essay on
Joyce. There Beckett also referred to Joyce's work as
"purgatorial," in the sense of "the absolute absence of
the Absolute" (22). Both references suggest the atmosphere of mundane "waiting" implicit in the indecision and doubt concerning absolutes. His
"tramps" are in Belacqua's state, of "waiting" for di-
rectives; a lifetime or a succession of them, since the

lines dividing one lifetime from another are not always clearly drawn.

Setting aside Belacqua's not very distinctly understood expectations of his eventual admission to Purgatory, Beckett's people are not unlike Belacqua: they are plagued by uncertainty, by "waiting," by a wearisome living through and out of life. On several occasions, as Strauss has pointed out, the waiting is a not undesirable state. The thought of passively enduring a repetition of the life cycle is not unattractive. Beckett has his Murphy think of "this post-mortem situation" with pleasure and gratification; Belacqua's situation is enviable: "rock and his embryonal repose, looking down at dawn across the reeds to the trembling of the austral sea and the sun obliquing to the north as it rose, immune from expiation until he should have dreamed it all through again, with the downright dreaming of an infant, from the spermarium to the crematorium." [17] Murphy's chair, and the death that comes to him there, are not unlike a condition of repose, of being "folded on the shelf" for a lifetime and freed from the agonies of waiting and puzzling out why.

This may remind us of the distinction Beckett makes in his *Proust* between Habit and "the crises of being." The repose is constantly and most rudely interrupted by the slither and shoddy of the world itself. The heroism of Beckett's characters is in part in the "waiting" itself, since it can have no issue; but it also comes from their arduously struggling to break through their uncertainties, the "absolute absence of Absolutes." Strauss has succinctly put the difference between Belacqua's waiting and Beckett's: "The heroes of Beckett's universe *really* vegetate, and, since this fate is unendurable, they try to vegetate *ideally*, i.e., they persuade themselves that there *is* an ascent and wait for some sort of angel to beckon them on, like Dante's pilgrims. But the angel, the epiphany, never comes, and they finally return to real vegetation. Like the vegetable, they wilt and disintegrate."

More Pricks Than Kicks is Beckett's early experiment in the Belacqua experience. The hero delays decision concerning the meaning of life until, *in articulo mortis*, it is too late to decide. The young Belacqua has not nearly the intensity of response of Joyce's Stephen, on whom he is more or less based. He is undecided about love, and lacks both Stephen's passionate joy and his guilt in it. He escapes, evades, scarcely ever fully wants or commits himself to experience. There are no doctrinal means in his case for explaining human affairs, or for sanctioning them. The public house is Belacqua's "boulder," wherein he "waits."

The stories are written with a heavy and amateurish irony; Beckett is still a long way from the "I" of the trilogy, and the nature of Belacqua's "solipsism" is observed from this kind of vantage point: "My some time friend Belacqua enlivened the last phase of his solipsism, before he trod the line and began to relish the world, with the belief that *the best thing he had to do was to move constantly from place to place*." Even here, however, his persons are characteristically *in motion*: "He was pleased to think that he could give what he called the Furies the slip by merely setting himself in motion." [18] In the case of Dante's Belacqua, the issue is met in indolence; he will wait, while the sun moves. Beckett's persons move, and assume (at least in collaboration with it) the diurnal motion of the earth. Belacqua Shuah is alert to all suggestions that he commit himself to passion or deep feeling; the pub is his refuge, its "graceful curates flying from customer to customer" (*p. 52*).

In every case the fears and disturbances of Joyce's *Dubliners,* and the major ones of *Portrait,* are evaded or met by one form or another of indulgence. Joyce's "The Dead" is matched, in "A Wet Night," by pettish indulgence, and the story culminates (113–14) in the early morning hours of Christmas Day, in Belacqua's vomiting the "experience" upon the wet lawn before the Casa Alba. Having failed always to "affront his destiny," he is left with no experience that he can properly value. In "Love and Lethe," he and Ruby (whose "naturally romantic and idealistic temper" had been reduced to despair by the need for "waiting") climb the high hill to a suicide pact that fails to come off. As the gun goes off harmlessly, "a great turmoil of lip-blood sprang up in the breasts of our two young felons, so that they came together in inevitable nuptial" (137). "L'Amour et la Mort . . . n'est qu'une mesme chose" (138).

Belacqua does commit himself, not once but three times: to Lucy, who dies in two years after a disastrous accident; to Thelma Woggs, who cannot resist him because he is a poet (166); finally, to Smeraldina, who survives him. These marriages are scarcely positive acts of passion for him; he lets them happen, having earlier either moved away from passionate occasion or been inspired to them by perverse means. In the end, the viciousness of life itself catches up to him. He lies on a hospital cot, awaiting an operation to remove a tumor the size of a brick from the back of his neck (237). He could wish to have been either well bred or plucky; but he was in truth "an indolent bourgeois poltroon, very talented up to a point, but not fitted for private life in the best and brightest sense" (233). He does not survive by many hours this "conspiracy to destroy him, body and soul" (248).

In the coffin he appears, with a "timeless mock on

[his] face," but so surrounded by the frills and lace of death's décor that he looks "like a pantomime baby" (268). This is Beckett's mockery of Belacqua Shuah, who will undoubtedly now assume the foetal position of Dante's Belacqua, if indeed the coffin hasn't already provided him with a Better Graves and Gardens status. The irony is very heavy. The situation is ugly indeed. Beckett is not sure if he wants to sneer at the world through Belacqua or merely to condemn Belacqua himself. The elaborate parallel with Dante's figure, which survives this group of stories to be meaningfully used in the novels, is here almost a failure. Belacqua Shuah comes to no last-minute confession, only to a dim awareness of a "conspiracy" against him, of which the anesthetist's act is the last cunning stroke.

Neither *Echo's Bones* nor *More Pricks Than Kicks* offers more than the slightest evidence of the genius to come. Beckett is much too much in the shadow of other geniuses. Yet both the "protagonist" of *Echo's Bones* and Beckett's Belacqua suggest, in a very artificial and imitative way it is true, the disfranchised person: the one, a Waste Land figure who does not have the moral strength to understand his disbelief; the other, an immature mixture of Dostoevsky's undergroundling, Goncharov's Oblomov (if we can imagine an Oblomov as a "man in motion away from life"), and Joyce's Dedalus. The spiritual crises of all three are present in dilution here and there in *More Pricks Than Kicks*; but there is nothing present in these stories to make the situation really critical. And, as we already know, Beckett does not deal in crises, physical or spiritual. These early pieces show him aware of, even sensitive to, the crises as determined in Eliot and Joyce; but they are not done in the spirit to suggest that Beckett was convinced of them.

Of the helplessness of *l'homme moyen sensuel* he was entirely aware, as well as of the best means of committing it to modern writing. His sensitivity to the pathos and confusion of the residual "thinking thing" of Dublin, London, Paris, and nowhere enabled him to follow along the lines of a freshly new record of his *cogito*. The failure in Beckett's eyes is not one of belief, nor is it a disaster that has come about through lack of a sustaining myth. It is quite simply a failure of definition, of the "language of the self." The fragments of rationality, of theory, of maxim and axiom and decorum, which the characters of his mature work try so frantically to put together and patch together, do not lend themselves either to Waste Land rhetoric or to elaborate aesthetic speculation. Instead, they lead to pathos and comedy: to those qualities inhering in the spectacle of the self aware of steady disintegration and fighting it in desperate assertion and inquiry.

BECKETT's *Murphy* (1938) begins in a world of "the nothing new" (*p. 1*). It is in many respects a record of very old, traditional issues, and of ancient means of solving them. It is also a comic novel, in the tradition of the buffoon of pathos, striving for an adjustment to a situation that is beyond his powers of tolerance but within the range of his rationalizing intellect. The resolution is *in intellectu*; it is also in terms of a homemade, improvisational mysticism. Like all other Beckett characters, Murphy has reasons for doing what he does, and these reasons are persuasive and engaging.

The "nothing new" of his world argues a rock-bottom situation. Murphy's needs are elemental, though not instinctively felt. He is discovered, in London, in "a medium-sized cage of north-western aspect commanding an unbroken view of medium-sized cages of south-eastern aspect" (1). There is, in short, no view at all; the physical aspect is dreary indeed, boxed in and geometric and impoverished. However, Murphy is not like the characters of Beckett's later novels. He commands both an inner and an outer prospect, and he is able clearly to differentiate between them. The inner world is not merely a "retreat" from the outer. Nor does he remove to it simply for reasons of timidity, but from a firm conviction of its self-evident superiority.

When his rather less than beloved Celia first discovers him, Murphy is lying face down on the floor of his "cage," his rocking chair—to which he is bound by scarves—on top of him. "Losing no time in idle speculation Celia undid the scarves and prised the chair off him with all possible speed. Part by part he subsided, as the bonds that held him fell away, until he lay fully prostrate in the crucified position, heaving." (28)

In this variant of the pratfall, Murphy's imperfections are initially seen. He is, after all, a fallible human, a prisoner of his body, which is in turn a prisoner in its "cage." The comic paradox is simply this: that Murphy seeks repose according to a fixed set of principled determinations. They are both philosophical and literary: a homespun Cartesian rationale, a faith in the ante-Purgatory of Belacqua. These are not mutually exclusive but complementary. In neither does Murphy speculate upon the existence of a supreme being. He is not interested in God; for while God has been assumed in the Cartesian universe, He is out of Murphy's reach, and he must therefore improvise his own extensions of self beyond mortal limits.

One may speculate upon Murphy's antecedents: in Dostoevsky's underground, Goncharov's Oblomov, Joyce's Leopold Bloom. The line of descent is there, but Murphy is uniquely a Beckett hero whose literary heritage is indifferently small. He is a reductive agent who brings both theological and metaphysical issues down to the simple devices of body, using matter to escape both. He argues indispensably the separation of body and mind. In stressing mind, Murphy hopes to overcome expected limitations of body. Interrupting his attempt to communicate with infinity, Celia has brought him a large black envelope which contains his *schema universalis*, his "thema Coelis" compiled by Ramaswami Krishnaswami Narayanaswami Suk. This proves a guide both to a specific finitude and to its link with infinity, to which Murphy is peculiarly and individually heir. (32–33)

The principles of Murphy's life are inordinately simple. They are sensed by him, exposited by others. Both Neary and Wylie, compatriots in Dublin, explain the "Doctrine of the Limit." It argues, to begin with, a clear dualism: Matter extended simply compounds itself and inflames the appetite for extension; the "quantum of wantum" (57) compounds, is invariable, is self-destructive. But the proportions remain fixed. " 'Humanity is a well with two buckets,' said Wylie, 'one going down to be filled, the other coming up to be emptied' " (58). The escape is through impelling the mind, through forcing a way into its infinite extension. Murphy doubts the veritable meaning of infinity, and will settle for a measurement that is at least comparable to it in provoking the imagination. The rocking chair, the scarves which bind, the absolute or nearly absolute repose, the rhythm of swaying back and forth, the dim light fading into darkness are all means of moving from matter to the clear spaces of mind. Suffusing all are the nuances of shadow and darkness which represent the transition from corporeality to transcendence. "There was not much light, the room devoured it, but [Celia] kept her face turned to what there was. The small single window condensed its changes, as half-closed eyes see the finer values of tones, so that it was never quiet in the room, but brightening and darkening in a slow ample flicker that went on all day, brightening against the darkening that was its end. A peristalsis of light, worming its way into the dark." (66)

Celia has other plans for Murphy. She is ambitious for him, wants him to be "respectable." She is his link to "blooming buzzing confusion" (29). But while Murphy goes out into it, on his perfunctory job-hunting, she is herself seduced by the ritual of the rocking chair. It is, after all, a symbol superior to the Market, "where the frenzied justification of life as an end to means threw light on Murphy's prediction, that livelihood would destroy one or two or all three of his life's goods" (67). Despite everything, she began to understand his purposes, while he—in search of a specious respectability—simply testified to the error of hers: "He had not the right gem to ensure success, indeed he had no gem of any kind" (75).

Instead, Murphy's ambitions are limited to Belacqua's "post-mortem situation." Not confident of his powers of circumventing mortality, Murphy chooses the rocking chair and Belacqua's shelf in ante-Purgatory. He visualizes the "embryonal repose" of Dante's friend,

> looking down at dawn across the reeds to the trembling of the austral sea and the sun obliquing to the north as it rose, immune from expiation until he should have dreamed it all through again, with the downright dreaming of an infant, from the spermarium to the crematorium. He thought so highly of this post-mortem situation, its advantages were present in such detail to his mind, that he actually hoped he might live to be old. Then he would have a long time lying there dreaming, watching the dayspring run through its zodiac, before the toil up hill to Paradise. (78)

There is something curiously untheological in this adaptation of Dante's vision. Murphy has reduced the role of God and His religion to a condition beyond himself; they are integers in a larger calculus, but he would prefer a metaphor which describes a means of postponing their responsibility. That God will manifest Himself to Murphy is a definite prospect, but He has no record of intervening in quotidian meditations. Murphy's status is an anticipation of that enjoyed by subsequent Beckett heroes. They are at once engaged in puzzling over the resources of the body for continuance and for resisting decay, in meditation over available notions of creativity, in prolonging existence in the very act of defining it. Murphy's Belacqua fancy is, therefore, an early speculation over the problem of "waiting for Godot."

There is no denying that Murphy is a "religious man," but this phrase must be understood in the Beckett lexicon. He is religious, as was Joyce's Bloom, in being intensely and nervously interested in last things—above all, in seeking the repose that must come to all men with the resolution of human ambivalences and grotesqueries. But he is religious within limits; one feels that secularism is closing in on him and that rational persuasions concerning transcendence are a long way toward deterioration. This "seedy solipsist" (82) maneuvers his way through the intricacies of an ordinary life, minutely calculating his petty advantages and taking minuscule risks to gain time and remain upright (or, better, right side up). He has the clown's appearance and his view of metaphysics; he counts the specks of dust in the beam of light he has tried to sweep into a dustpan.

Murphy's chief opportunity is given him through lucky chance. He is hired on a temporary basis in the Magdalen Mental Mercyseat, a haven for distraught egos. It is the ultimate refuge from the blooming buzz; Suk had warned him to "Avoid exhaustion by speech,"

because he had been blessed with "Intense Love
nature prominent, rarely suspicioning the Nasty, with
inclinations to Purity" (32). The contrast of sanity
and lunacy is implied; Murphy goes his own way in
defining each, and the inhabitants of the M.M.M. are,
almost all of them, "sane" if the word means anything
at all. Beckett's descriptions of lunacy follow a time-
honored habit: The "bright spirits" are inside, having
withdrawn to the inside from the chaos outside.
Those who are not in are either sadist exploiters of
those who are or spirits trying to resolve the antino-
mies of the outside.

Within the M.M.M., imperfect as they seem, are
the resources for quiet meditation. Beckett, aware
that Murphy's new position will encourage speculation, pauses in chapter six to describe his mind, or
rather his mind as "it felt and pictured itself to be." It
seemed to him "a large hollow sphere, hermetically
closed to the universe without." It was not therefore
deprived, but rather enjoyed the advantage of dualistic
immunity. "Nothing ever had been, was or would be
in the universe outside it but was already present as
virtual, or actual, or virtual rising into actual, or actual
falling into virtual, in the universe inside it." (107)
Dualism therefore encouraged warm inner meditation, immune from the "blooming buzzing confusion," since "the mental experience was cut off from
the physical experience, its criteria were not those of
the physical experience, the agreement of part of its
content with physical fact did not confer worth on
that part." (108)

The splitting of body from mind has its own
pathos, but it is also an inestimable advantage. The
very frailty of the body encouraged experiments in
transcendence. Though there was intercourse between
body and mind, Murphy did not find it a matter of

supreme concern: "He neither thought a kick because he felt one nor felt a kick because he thought one." There was perhaps "a non-mental non-physical Kick from all eternity, simply revealed to Murphy in its correlated modes of consciousness and extension, the kick *in intellectu* and the kick *in re*. But where then was the supreme Caress?" He was not much disturbed about the possibility of "supernatural determination," but devoted his efforts to exploiting the advantages of the dualism. This task involved underrating the body and setting up its physical circumstances as nearly ideally suited to meditation, protecting the mind from the risk of its suffering the "vicissitudes of the body." (109)

Pursuing this aim, Murphy finds himself again and again in need of physical rest—a surcease of movement—so that the threat to the mind is not actualized. Murphy's aging may therefore be described as a gradual achievement of relief from the troubles of matter in motion. The progress toward quiescence is described in terms of three zones: light, half light, dark. In the first there are forms with parallels in matter; a basic curiosity in Beckett's men has to do with the physical bodies, illuminated in more or less intensity, which occupy spaces, or "the elements of physical experience available for a new arrangement." (*111*) In the half light are "the forms without parallels." Here the light recedes, leaving the grey which is Beckett's dominant color. To move away from the light that defines objects, into the dusk that neutralizes them, is to enter an area of twilight pleasure, "the Belacqua bliss and others scarcely less precise." These are pleasures in unextended being—that is, without spatial location and arrangement. They are what Murphy seeks in his rocking chair, but they are transitional to the third, the condition of "non-Newtonian motion": no objects, no space, but "a flux of forms, a perpetual coming together and falling asunder of forms." (112)

Taking these three conditions in order, one may say that the first involves the risk of body (corruption, growing weakness, the move toward death); the second is a state of obscurity but relaxation from danger; the third is an absolute condition, in which the responsibilities of body are totally surrendered, and an absolute freedom reigns of unobstructed forms. The rocking-chair rhythms are transitional; the scarves fix his body, so that it will not irrelevantly move. Above all, these speculations require warmth. Murphy refuses to help his friend Ticklepenny unless he will be given heat. Considerable ingenuity is required before a gas-jet in the w.c. can be used to bring warmth to Murphy's garret. Within it and the wards of M.M.M., the heat and the forms (of the mind) assault their inhabitants.

The wards themselves have a suggestive design: they hint weakly of sacrifice and the metaphors of theology, but they bespeak principally of bodily deterioration, the rags and abscesses of a deficient humanity: "The wards consisted of two long corridors, intersecting to form a T, or more correctly a decapitated potence, the three extremities developed into spacious crutch-heads, which were the reading-, writing- and recreation-rooms or 'wrecks,' known to the wittier ministers of mercy as the sublimatoria." (166)

One needs to observe that, in all of this semicomic history, there is also a deep pathos. Beckett is giving us in this early novel a prior view of his disinherited and disenchanted world. The comedy is in appearances, but the appearances are themselves pathetic because they assume the lowest common denominator of dignity and human resources. The great majority of the patients "preferred simply to hang about doing nothing" (166). This "nothing" is one of the three forms of negation in Beckett's work: it is the "nothing new" to which Murphy awakens in the beginning; it is the nothing in which Vladimir and Estragon exist in *Waiting for Godot*, trying to fill it or to "occupy" it, by any means at their disposal; but it is also the void to which the defective Cartesian mind aspires, the semidarkness of Belacqua's waiting, the total darkness of Murphy's free forms.

The comedian-victim of the M.M.M. is in basic rapport with Murphy. Not only does he not mind being their male nurse; he enjoys the task. He shares their fears of the "nothing new"; but each of them has, like him, sought the merciful, stasis refuge from the "blooming buzzing confusion." Murphy's fate is to be destroyed by an accident which occurs to the mechanism of the Cartesian W.C. The gas-jet, formerly used to light the way to a universal sewer, now linked by a series of wires and chains to Murphy's radiator, falls apart, and Murphy is translated entirely from this world to the next, his bodily substance turned to ashes, which are in turn accidentally distributed over the floor of a London pub (275).

So endeth Murphy, always suspicious of the capacities of physical substance to sustain the mind, now entirely lost in the detritus of space. In his life he had diligently avoided the confused inadequacies of the world, but he was at last to fall victim to a "mechanical mistake" and his ashes let loose because of human error. The novel admirably points to archetypal subheroics. The Beckett man is engaged restlessly in an undiminished effort to define himself; the physical odds against him increase as the energy of his effort grows. He is a prisoner of the rusting cage of his body, the dispiriting "underground" of his habitation. He does not defy reason but gingerly though unavailingly uses it. He ends in something less and more than disaster. The suspicion is that what he is striving to define is "nothing," and that what he is "waiting for" is annihilation. But he can't go on, he must go on, he will go on, and at the same time puzzles over the meaning of can't, must, and will.

ii

Watt (written in 1944, but not published until 1953) is an epistemological farce. What Murphy tries to accomplish by rhythms and stillness, Watt seeks through talk. His peculiar rationality is a stuck-needle Cartesianism, in which the possibilities of language and reason are exploited nervously and feverishly. As Jacqueline Hoefer has described it,[1] "His mind appears to be a kind of untiring logic-machine which dutifully reshuffles into seemingly endless logical combinations the scanty facts of physical experience which Watt's senses supply."

Further, the mystery of Beckett's naming is given an interesting nudge. Watt is clearly a pun on What, as the master he appears to serve is Knott, a Joycean fusion of itself with Not; so that the Watt-Knott of the novel is at the center of its speculation, Watt offering the processes of inquiry and Knott the ambiguous nonanswer. Knott also occasionally seems to suggest the evasive confusion of Kafka's *The Castle*. He leaves unanswered the questions of his existence and the manner in which he should or might be served. Does he "not" exist, or is the matter of his existence a "knotty" mystery? But Knott is after all in part the product of Watt's rationality; in trying to define himself, Watt "creates" Knott, so that he may serve him and in serving him justify himself. *Ex nihilo nil*. The substance of Knott is nothing if not contained in Watt's mind.

Speculation concerning Beckett's namings is a fatal temptation. The W of Watt's name is an inverted M; we leave the M of Murphy's Magdalen Mental Mercyseat (where he occupies a "chair," in which he is finally discovered dead), to encounter the W of *Watt*. Subsequently, we encounter Molloy, Moran, Malone, other, minor creations (Mahood, Macmann, etc.); but Malone's name is itself one of two words, in the only title of Beckett's novels that has two substantial words: *Malone Meurt*. The *eur* sound joins the *ur* of Murphy, or approximately; the *or* of Moran is the sound of the noun *Mort* to which *Meurt* belongs as verb. The n sound of Knott is like the double n of *The Unnamable*. In this last-named novel, The Unnamable, who is either each of all the others or the creator of all of them, or no-name, thinks of his final "creation" as Worm. And in *Worm* all of the implications in the other names are contained: the *or* of Mort, the W of Watt, the m (which is here the last letter of a word that represents the full span from *womb* to *tomb*, or from *spermarium* to *crematorium*). If The Unnamable is the creator of all these, he is also linked to Knott, *ex nihilo nil*, or the "god-given godhead" of what Joyce calls this "farraginous chronicle."

These echoes and conjunctions suggest a dispossessed Adam, or an *homme isolé* who is responsible for his own creations, yet ultimately puzzled and confused by them. An atmosphere of uncertainty (Beckett's "absolute absence of Absolutes") dominates the scene. Each of Beckett's characters improvises existences (his own, God's, the world's) as he goes on; he must improvise as well his relationships to these improvisations. As The Unnamable begins by saying,

"Where now? Who now? When now? . . . keep going, going on, call that going, call that on" (*Three Novels, p. 401*).

But these elaborations are scarcely all evident in *Watt*. Beckett's hero is here engaged in an intense though limited meditation. It involves the statement of all possible rational combinations and possibilities and the selection of none. As Christine Brooke-Rose has so ably put it,[2] the "weird almost mathematical style in *Watt* [is] a style with a slightly legal flavour, a style based on permutations of possibilities. For not only does any one action have numerous explanations, but metaphysically speaking there are also numerous other possible actions which, though not actualized by us in any one instance, exist nevertheless in a timeless mind." Above all, *Watt* is a testimony of language, a comedy of *je parle*. The physical setting is not nearly so elaborate as that of *Murphy*; nor is there any of the melodrama that heightens the earlier book. Later in his career, Beckett was to write "Acts without Words"; here he gives us, almost, a words-without-acts equivalent.

Watt is on the edge of being the caricature comedian. His smile makes a doubtful impression: "To many it seemed a simple sucking of the tooth."[3] He had an elaborately precise and deliberate walk, a "funambulistic stagger" (*p. 31*).

Watt's way of advancing due east, for example, was to turn his bust as far as possible towards the north and at the same time to fling out his right leg as far as possible towards the south and at the same time to fling out his left leg as far as possible towards the north, and then again to turn his bust as far as possible towards the north and to fling out his left leg as far as possible towards the south, and so on, over and over again, many

many times, until he reached his destination, and could sit down. (30)

This is the mechanical action of the clownish tight-rope walker, or of the comedian who plays a drunk try-ing to describe the sober straight line. Unaccountably, Lady McCann, perhaps exasperated by the twisting, jerky motion, throws a stone which lands on Watt's hat and then falls to the ground—a providential escape, for Watt has a poor-healing skin. But he takes no notice of the aggression and walks on as though it has not happened (32). This reaction, like others, is typical of Watt's denial of what happens outside his mind. He is adamantly fixed within the habits of his mind, and his actions and deliberations are a testi-mony to a diligent self-possession. When he arrives at his destination, he feels the joy of all-in-one-piece identity:

> When in a word he will be in his midst at last, after so many years spent clinging to the perimeter. These first impressions, so hardly won, are undoubtedly delicious. What a feeling of security! They are transports that few are spared, nature is so exceedingly accommodating, on the one hand, and man, on the other. . . . He re-moves his hat without misgiving, he unbuttons his coat and sits down, proffered all pure and open to the long joys of being himself, like a basin to a vomit. (41)

Watt tries to match his words to the physical con-fusion about him, exploring his world in detail, "mil-lions of little things moving all together out of their old place, into a new one nearby, and furtively, as though it was forbidden" (43). In truth, Watt's actions are a mechanical repetition of "the whole bloody" quotidian business (47). "The ordinary per-son eats a meal, then rests from eating for a space, then eats again, then rests again, then eats again, then rests again, then eats again, then rests again, then eats again, then rests again, and in this way, now eating, now resting from eating, he deals with the difficult problem of hunger, and indeed I think I may add thirst, to the best of his ability and according to his state of fortune." (52)

This set of acts is a design of humdrum, which is matched by a torrent of talk and debate, the question shredding the reality into minute parts, dividing and classifying trivial combinations of practical and rational possibility. Watt moves funambulistically, in his mind as in his body: he queries identity in the act of practicing it. The deliberate application of his mind to the most trivial problems leads to the larger question of self as a composite of trivialities that in turn leads to the still larger question of God, or Watt is Knott. In so moving toward the definition of the ultimate certainty, Watt offers an ingenious view of rational creativity: "For the only way one can speak of nothing is to speak of it as though it were something, just as the only way one can speak of God is to speak of him as though he were a man, which to be sure he was, in a sense, for a time, and as the only way one can speak of man, even our anthropologists have realised that, is to speak of him as though he were a termite." (77)

In the service of Knott, Watt speculates upon the Watt-ness of Knott's pots; the true nature of potness escapes him, and "it was just this hairbreadth departure from the truth that so excruciated Watt" (81). And his need of "semantic succour" was at times so great "that he would set to trying names on things, and on himself, almost as a woman hats" (83). For Watt's struggle is with the knowledge of phenomena, and of its flow of succession and repetition: "for the coming is in the shadow of the going and the going is in the shadow of the coming, that is the annoying part of it" (57).

The net effect of Watt's deliberations is that of a circle in search of its center; he thinks himself as center, but is not sure, so that the process is an endless enclosing of circles moving about centers. As Miss Hoefer has said in her *Perspective* article (*p.* 176), "A circle seems to be the right symbol for Watt's world, for it so forcefully asserts a limit—solipsistic, self-contained, and inescapable." He observes reality, but only to deny it as existing except in terms of his "system," which consists of a succession of prattle: "Je parle sans cesse; donc je suis, peut-être." So, in considering the picture in Erskine's room, he thinks it to represent "a circle and its centre in search of each other, or a circle and its centre in search of a centre and a circle respectively" (129).

In some respects, this is a parody of the pretentious rhetoric and delusive logic of conventional philosophical thinking, using words and concepts as a clown uses balls or the circles of a bicycle. Watt's deliberate rhetoric, as his name, is as much a comic inversion of conventional talk as is the speech of Lucky (*Waiting for Godot*) or the stock-in-trade of Ionesco's plays. There is an important difference, however. Watt is in earnest; his rigmarole is an honest attempt to define the wattness of things as he can both apprehend them and participate in them. He goes all the way, to become involved in an elaborate consideration, first of the reality of things, then of the reality of the words he uses to define their possibilities, finally of their source and cause.

iii

Beckett has claimed that his best work, all that he values, was written between 1945 and 1950.[4]

This would exclude *Murphy* and *Watt* but include the trilogy of novels, three *nouvelles* and the *Textes pour rien*. He underestimates the value of his first two novels, as comic creations and as anticipations of major concerns in the trilogy. There are some conspicuous changes: The trilogy is directly narrated by its characters (the "I" becomes extraordinarily complex as the certainty of self-definition diminishes); they are less involved in the rudiments and more concerned over ultimate questions of being; in being less clearly and overtly characterized, they are more complex and their feverish search for precision is a more powerful and moving engagement.

Here too, for the first time the full weight of the question of responsibility comes into play. The "I's" of the trilogy are a fluctuant mass of self, moving and fading and re-emerging as specific selves, diminishing and enforcing their strengths, as the strength of declamation and the power of doubt struggle for dominance. While *Murphy* and *Watt* are parodies of epistemological issues, the trilogy is directly involved with the question of being, creation, extension, corporeality, and with the several languages of assertion and doubt.

Throughout, the "I's" of the trilogy alternate in the roles of creator and created. They take on themselves the full responsibilities of birth, movement, persistence in space, and decline. *Molloy* presents the problem of creation in its vital statement. Both its titular hero and Moran go on "quest journeys," in search of each other, with these objectives: to find their causes, to unite as aspects of the same self. There is a typical Beckettian doubt concerning precise place, *status quo* and *terminus ad quem*. The characters also diminish, become less and less self-certain, gradually lose their wholeness of being, as they proceed toward each other.

Both are creators, as each imagines or projects himself into relationships with others; both are also "machines" or "men-using-machines," the "Cartesian
centaurs" of which Hugh Kenner speaks. The bicycle,
the crutch, the stick, become spatial adjuncts of the
body; the mind projects as the body diminishes. As
are the other members of the trilogy, *Molloy* is a
drama of cognition and creation, as opposed to the
traditional representation of characters involved in
plot. This change, as we have seen, had a long history
before Beckett applied his special talents to it: Joyce's
Bloom (and particularly Bloom-Stephen of the Circe
episode) and his Earwicker ("Here Comes Every-
body," "Haveth Childers Everywhere"), Proust's
Marcel. Modern literature is abundantly supplied
with instances of the epistemological quest.

While *Murphy* and *Watt* may be considered Beckett's final exercises in shedding the Joycean influence,
Molloy is pure and primary Beckett. The opening
pages resort to elementary questions of origin and
cause. "I began at the beginning" in "my mother's
room," and the first question has to do with the biological versus the creative source of being. Beyond
that, there is the question of going on, that "rumor rising at birth and even earlier, what shall I do? . . .
And to follow?" Molloy speculates about another being, who is identified in part two as Moran, searching
for and merging with Molloy. He peers through the
haze of a dimly seen ante-Purgatory, at "Belacqua, or
Sordello, I forget." The mother is after all a trivial
cause; Molloy seeks a father or a self's self. "But in
spite of my soul's leap out to him, at the end of its
elastic, I saw him only darkly, because of the dark and
then because of the terrain, in the folds of which he
disappeared from time to time, to re-emerge further
on, but most of all I think because of other things

calling me and towards which one after the other my soul was straining, wildly." [5]

This passage may almost be taken for Beckett's primary text: the creature straining to see and to define his creator, at the same time straining towards "others," who are either creators or creatures; the mélange of relationships undecided and ill-defined; and at the heart of the quest the "I," who is, at least for a definable moment a person (that is, a possible soul with a physical parallel in material substance). Beyond this there is the confusion of times, of "several different occasions," so that the relationships are not even spatially secure: "And perhaps it was A one day at one place, then C another at another, then a third the rock and I, and so on for the other components, the cows, the sky, the sea, the mountains." (*pp. 13–14*)

These are major concerns because Molloy was not "caused" in birth, or cannot believe he was. His mother had had him when she was very young, so that they are now both old crones, "sexless, unrelated" (17). His relationship with her is comical, indifferent: "I know she did all she could not to have me" (19), and she'd jostled him during the prenatal months and thus "spoiled the only endurable, just endurable, period of my enormous history" (19–20). But he rejects the mother not because he resents her but because his is an epistemological not a biological question; the matter of the "spermarium" is, after all, simple and minor. The fact is that she had not succeeded in getting him unstuck and he was therefore destined for "less compassionate sewers" (19). Setting aside the womb as cause, Molloy turns to the less obvious and more bewildering issue of creation as artifact as opposed to accident. The fact is that he does exist, that he does have a body; the issue is not that, but has to do with self-definition, a question of the imaginative extension of matter in and through and beyond space.

Something of Watt adheres in Molloy. He speculates upon possibilities; he imposes language upon them. But, unlike Watt, he comes back to the fact of Molloy lying in the ditch, eating grass. As his physical members deteriorate (they do in all Beckett heroes, noticeably and painfully), Molloy turns to "machines." The crutch is an extension of the leg, or a substitute leg; and the motion crutches give the man becomes a "rapture," a "series of little flights, skimming the ground. You take off, you land, through the thronging sound in wind and limb, who have to fasten one foot to the ground before they dare lift up the other." (83) Motion begets motion; the paths described by the crutches go beyond definable places and immensely expand Molloy's world. But he is not sure if he carries himself or the world carries him (85). In any case, his powers of this kind are bound to diminish, for they depend upon a corruptible body, whose members will diminish and may disappear altogether. Death is a condition Molloy finds it hard to accept, "a condition I have never been able to conceive to my satisfaction" (88).

He has recourse to both Murphy's and Watt's devices for circumventing it: trying first, in a sea voyage, to transcend bodily limits; then, in an obsessive rational concern over the relationship of pebbles to pockets, to force existence into a language and logic of trivial choices: "And sitting on the shore, before the sea, the sixteen stones spread out before my eyes, I gazed at them in anger and perplexity" (92). But the stones are themselves forms, and their disposition in his pockets is a challenging symmetry. Molloy would think ideally of "sixteen pockets, symmetrically dis-

posed, each one with its stone. . . . This would have
freed me from all anxiety, not only within each cycle
taken separately, but also for the sum of all cycles,
though they went on forever. . . . And it was above
all inelegant in this, to my mind, that the uneven distribution was painful to me, bodily." (96–97)

This question of symmetry, balance, and "elegance"
is of the essence in Molloy's development. As a body
he is not distinguished; in relation to his mother he
bores himself and she him; beyond these are the
questions of his having been more substantially
created, by himself or some other, or that some other
and he have mutually obliged. If this last, then the
qualities of the mind become the saving grace, and the
matter of cycles, choices, languages, decisions, is pre-
eminent.[6]

Above all in Molloy's journey, there is the question
of physical pain. He disintegrates before our eyes,
having at first a bicycle which magnificently extends
his power of motion; then, crutches, whose assistance
in motion temporarily give him an exhilarating, almost a metaphysical strength. But they too depend on
relatively sound members, or at least members of
which they may be accessories. When they are gone,
they leave the agony and monotony of painful crawling, like a secular, a reduced, motion along the stations of the cross. "But I am human, I fancy, and my
progress suffered, from this state of affairs, and from
the slow and painful progress it had always been,
whatever may have been said to the contrary, was
changed, saving your presence, to a veritable calvary,
with no limit to its stations and no hope of crucifixion." (103)

Pain is an inheritance of the body, and cannot be
explained away, and was not by Descartes. For
Molloy, the two kinds of pain are the "monotonous"

and the "variable," and both of these (though the second is the more "heroic") lead to skepticism, most of all to the fear that God does not exist, or that if He does the fact is of little consequence, or that in any case He "will not come." The strategy of life reduces itself to a "going on" and a "waiting"; and Beckett moves further and further from a justification of the worth of either.[7] Molloy convinces himself that he must go on, though he cannot say why. "But it is forbidden to give up and even to stop an instant. So I wait, jogging along, for the bell to say, Molloy, one last effort, it's the end. That's how I reason, with the help of images little suited to my situation. And I can't shake off the feeling, I don't know why, that the day will come for me to say what is left of all I had." (107–8)

Both Molloy and Moran begin in a state of comparative soundness (they both bear testimony to existence), then proceed toward self-disintegration, as they move toward each other and toward mutual identity. Edith Kern speaks of Moran as the creator of both Watt and Murphy, though Molloy is "a part of him," not just a creature but inseparably identified with Moran.[8] They are not "separate phases" of a greater creation, but bear the same burdens and suffer the same painful deterioration of body and spirit. If a difference may be cited, it is that Moran is more conspicuously the creative imaginer, the "fabulous artificer," Molloy more given to meeting emergencies by improvisation.

Jacques Moran begins in full and arbitrary command of his faculties. This is simply to say that he is more confident of the rational life than he should be, and is subsequently punished by declining further than Molloy because he has a longer way to go. "I had a methodical mind and never set out on a mission without prolonged reflection as to the best way of setting out. It was the first problem to solve, at the outset of each enquiry." (130–31) This firmness has in it nevertheless the seed of doubt, and Moran's confidence is "beset by enemies" that are in themselves products of his imagination. The rationalist mind, of which Moran is one of Beckett's more interesting specimens, suppresses doubts, or ignores their causes, but they remain nevertheless, and return to haunt and damage him.

He begins in the full Cartesian confidence, subsides, finds that he can pierce "the outer turmoil's veil"; going out, "I drown in the spray of phenomena" (148). But his real crisis is Molloy, as pain was Descartes'. In a sense Moran is a symbolic compensation for Descartes' errors of omission. He applies "principles" to the question of Molloy and his pain: there are five Molloys, he says, the fifth "that out of Youdi"; the other four are "He that inhabited me, my caricature of same, Gaber's and the man of flesh and blood somewhere awaiting me" (154). That is, there are five creative acts whose products are Molloy; each of the creators is part of a scheme of creation, at least at first responsibly initiated by Moran. But this is to substitute rationalization for reality: "how far [were] these Molloys constant and how far subject to variation" (155).

Moran is both creator and creature, artist and experiencing object, assailant and victim. He is, above all, as human creature, subject to the same physical deterioration as Molloy. When he lies ill in the wood, his leg paining him, he suffers exactly the same diminution of powers. He experiences visions of an "intruder self," which at once is Molloy and "vaguely resembled my own" (204).

When he returns to his home, in pain and barely

able to move at all, the metamorphosis is complete. "Certain questions of a theological nature preoccupied me strangely. As for example. . . . 4. How much longer are we to hang about waiting for the antechrist? . . . 7. Does nature observe the sabbath? . . . 13. What was God doing with himself before the creation? 14. Might not the beatific vision become a source of boredom, in the long run? . . . 16. What if the mass for the dead were read over the living?" (227–28)

The notes, from which the above questions are taken, are a parody set of principles, directed against the rational order of statements and answers to questions found in Descartes. In the end, all has become doubt. Moran, on crutches now, is on the way to becoming Moran-Molloy: "My knee is no better. It is no worse either. I have crutches now. I shall go faster, all will go faster. There will be happy days. I shall learn." (239) *Molloy* ends in ambiguities, as it began in them: "Then I went into the house and wrote, It is midnight. The rain is beating on the windows. It was not midnight. It was not raining." (240)

iv

As *Molloy* ends in suffering, pain, and doubt, *Malone Dies* opens in the expectation of death: "I shall soon be dead at last in spite of all. . . . I could die today, if I wished, merely by making a little effort, if I could wish, if I could make an effort. But it is just as well to let myself die, quietly, without rushing things." [9] Malone is ostensibly an expression of Dostoevsky's underground man, but he is a passive figure, not in any way in rebellion against the world or using himself to flout the realms of conventional sense or reason. Nor is he Kafka's spirit brooding over legalistic intricacies of his moral obligation or in the self-hateful condition of Gregor Samsa. Malone simply "lies dying"; "I shall die tepid, without enthusiasm," he says (*p. 244*).

As such a man, Malone moves out from the first novel of the trilogy, an extension of the predicaments of Molloy-Moran. The trilogy is, quite simply and superficially stated, a portrayal of the loss of self. It begins with the impact of pain (and loss of members) upon self-confidence; it proceeds to explore the mind of a moribund; it ends upon the question of the total loss of name and of naming, of being and creativity. It ends very much as *Endgame* ends, were it considered a sequel of *Waiting for Godot*.

The matter of dying in Beckett's work is basically a question of self-inventory: Who is it that is dying? How may he identify himself if he is to die? How may he die "significantly"? In Malone's case, it is a matter of properties, of things with which he, as a dying being, can be identified, if it is to be known that it is he who has died and dying that has occurred to him. First in the inventory is the room in which he has been left to die, "a plain private room apparently, in what appears to be a plain ordinary house" (*248*). There are no mirrors, no Lisas or Sonias to remind him of a commiserating Christ, no one to explore his conscience with him or in spite of him. We have only a body lying on a bed, a stick, a pencil, some paper; there is a sense of a consciousness diminishing, but in this case, "the loss of consciousness for me was never any great loss" (*249*).

Malone suffers the customary Beckettian deprivation and has recourse to the usual contrivances for struggling against it. Since he has neither bicycle nor crutch, nor could use them if he had, he cannot assert himself spatially. Aside from the very useful stick and the indispensable pencil, he is reduced to elementals:

"What matters is eat and excrete. Dish and pot, dish and pot, these are the poles." (250) Even so, he antici- pates the time when even these sustaining functions will cease: "There is virtually nothing [my body] can do" (253).

He has recourse to the mind. The mind always re- mains, in Beckett's world, long after the body has ceased being endurable. He will write his memoirs, create a succession of beings to whom he can attach himself and thus be in a sense responsible for an existence. The experiment is engaging but it has its low moments: "what tedium," he says after an espe- cially uninspiring exercise (257). Further, the creation which is the memoir and the fact which is his mori- bund present self are not always convincingly the same; the exercises in re-creation are interspersed by moments of isolation, "the old dark gathering, the solitude preparing, by which I know myself" (257). "But I know what darkness is, it accumulates, thick- ens, then suddenly bursts and drowns everything" (258–59). Even the act of creation is uncertain; the words "slip, slide, . . . perish"; they "run riot in my head, pursuing, flying, clashing, merging, endlessly" (270).

Actually, the fact of existence is only palliated by the imagination. Malone has frequently to come back to elementary functions and sounds: pains that "seem new to me," the feel and sound of sucking. These impressions are all parodic versions of the *cogito: I* suck, therefore I am, etc.; "The search for myself is ended." (271) But it is more than a deterioration of the *res cogitans*, because unconsciousness threatens and when it occurs epistemological questions will vanish: "I was time, I devoured the world. Not now, any more. A man changes. As he gets on." (275) In the end the only formula left will be *Malone meurt*.

The process of dying itself has its generalizing effects: his life had been full of a buzzing of sounds, a spray of phenomena. Age generalizes them, into "one vast continuous buzzing. The volume of sound perceived remained the same. I simply had lost the faculty of decomposing it." (282–83)

Meanwhile the other Malone egos are drawn out of his mind: Saposcat, Lambert the pig butcher, others. But they do not cohere and in any case the words he uses to define them produce "moral tedium" (297). He returns to this room and this place: perhaps it is, after all, already a tomb, "and this space which I take to be the street in reality no more than a wide trench with other vaults opening upon it." The question of his present state is prompted by the tedium of the memoirs and by the suspicion that this basement is after all a tomb, with "tiers of basements one on top of another." (299)

But this decline of confidence alternates with moments of revival. Malone is sure there are other people in this house, and that life is going on. But is any of this real? It is just as likely that "in reality all that is perhaps nothing but my worms" (301). For example, the room has no real light or color, except "in so far as this kind of grey incandescence may be called a color." He himself, he says, "emits grey." (302) If his worst doubts are realized, he and his pencil are really engaged in a Poe-esque dialogue, an act in cerements and not a ceremony. In any case, the pencil has diminished so that it is now almost useless; very soon there won't be enough of it to hold (305).

These speculations lead naturally to the doubt that he had in fact been born. However he may answer that question, "I shall go on doing as I have always done, not knowing what it is I do, nor who I am, nor where I am, nor if I am" (309). Beyond the tedium,

the doubt, the painful sense of moribundity, there is
that resolve (it dominates, as an "affirmative note,"
Beckett's stories and plays); but it must constantly be
renewed and checked. Its natural ally is the figure of
Macmann, third creature-surrogate of Malone. Macmann, while he stands in the same relationship to
Malone as the others, is an assertion beyond being
merely an invention. Like Malone in aging, he is
nevertheless alive and standing straight, and in love
with another creature, Moll, a "little old woman, im-
moderately ill-favoured of both face and body" (353).
She wears for earrings two long ivory crucifixes, which
"swayed wildly at the least movement of her head"
(353). They are the thieves; "Christ is in my mouth,"
a "long yellow canine bared to the roots and carved,
with the drill probably, to represent the celebrated
sacrifice." (363) Christ as creator has been reduced to
occupying a cave, an opening, an orifice, from which
life or its blasphemous facsimile emerges or should
emerge. Molly Bloom also associates love with crucifixes; and Molly will sometime become Moll, one-
toothed and offering love *in extremis.*

> *To the lifelong promised land*
> *Of the nearest cemetery*
> *With his Sucky hand in hand*
> *Love it is at last leads Hairy.* (361)

Both Moll and Macmann are, nevertheless, last-
breath exercises of Malone's imagination. The boredom and the exhaustion its efforts create will now
lead to last gasps: "To be dead, before her, on her,
with her, and turn, dead on dead, about poor mankind,
and never have to die any more, from among the
living" (363–64). Yet, he urges, "Try and go on"
(382). And he does, until spasms of dying and fitful
creation alternate in his last moments.

never there he will never
never anything
there
any more (398)

Malone dies, without a comma or a period to spare.
His creative energy has sputtered and died; the pencil
is gone, the stick lost, and he is himself no more than
expendable and corrupt body. In its alternation of
creative and dying gasps, *Malone Dies* is paradigmatic
of the "absolute absence of Absolutes" in Beckett's
work. His struggle to find and then to maintain identity is limited from the beginning to the possibilities
of a desperately inquiring mind and the diminishing
potencies of a dying animal.

v

The trilogy appropriately concludes with a
book called *The Unnamable*. "Unquestioning. I, say I.
Unbelieving." [10] *The Unnamable* is the extreme form
of the "un-novel"; facts established in paragraph one
of the traditional novel are here still in doubt at the
end. Vivian Mercier has said [11] concerning this question that "The Unnamable's interior monologue may
go on to infinity, for all we know. If it were to, we
might describe this novel as a curve having one of its
axes as an asymptote. In other words, as y (the length
of the novel) approached infinity, x (the content of
the novel) would approach nearer and nearer to zero.
Content zero, length infinity—these are the mathematical limits of the novel."

Together with this provocative idea of the anti-
novel's extension to an infinity of noncontent, there
is the fact of the babble itself; it is like the meaningful
nonsense of the talking clown, and it bears a philosophical resemblance to the silent-picture antics of
Buster Keaton, occasionally of Charlie Chaplin. In

his *Spectrum* article (*p. 9*), Hugh Kenner speaks of it as "an anxious audible dumb-show . . . immaculate solipsism compelled to talk, talk, talk, and fertile in despairing explanations for its own garrulity." In this sense, *The Unnamable* is a lineal descendant of *Watt*, as an epistemological comedy. The gravely serious import of it, however, lies in the belief that—assuming nothing else to be certain—to talk is the only guarantee of identity. The talk is itself loaded with the contradictions which a rudderless self-assertion promotes. In *The Unnamable* the self reaches, not its logical conclusion, but as Kenner says (*p. 22*), "the centre of the solitary world."

The determination of Molloy to "go on" at all costs, Malone's decision to persist, Moran's pushing his inquiry beyond the conventional setting in which he begins—these are all contained and negated (they exist in a shell of their opposites) in The Unnamable's spew of meditation. The questions are real enough, and terribly important: Who am I, how do I relate to other objects, and do these objects exist outside me or are they product of my mind, if I have a mind, if I am I? They are not answered; negation almost catches up to assertion in this final novel. "The thing to avoid, I don't know why, is the spirit of System."

The Unnamable cannot be placed or defined. He is any and all of Beckett's M's and W's, and the negation of any and all of them. For example, Malone "passes before me at doubtless regular intervals, unless it is I who pass before him." But perhaps it is Molloy, who is wearing Malone's hat? (*403*) But could Molloy be here, without my knowledge? (*404*)

Then, as to the Where am I? This place: what is it and how big is it? "I like to think I occupy the centre, but nothing is less certain." (*406*) The basic figure of Beckett's work is the circle, or fraction thereof. Watt speculates upon a painting as depicting the circle in search of its center; Gogo and Didi describe circles, with hats, words, repetitions of scenes; Molloy, with crutches and oars; the single actor of "Acts without Words" moves ever toward and away from a circle of light, which continues to deceive him until he refuses to allow it; Krapp circles back again and again to a certain point in his "last tape." The Unnamable is preoccupied with circles, almost to the exclusion of all else. "In a sense I would be better off at the circumference, since my eyes are always fixed in the same direction. But I am certainly not at the circumference." (406–7) Perhaps the most provocative circular motion in Beckett's fiction is that described by Mahood's crutches, which make irregular loops around the earth. "And my course is not helicoidal, I got that wrong too, but a succession of irregular loops, now short and sharp as in the waltz, now of a parabolic sweep that embraces entire boglands, now between the two, somewhere or other, and invariably unpredictable in direction, that is to say determined by the panic of the moment." (452)

But Mahood is no longer capable of such movement, but only of rest, sitting within a jar outside a third-rate chop house, cared for by its mistress, who comes once a week to move him and "clean his residence." "Stuck like a sheaf of flowers in a deep jar, its neck flush with my mouth, on the side of a quiet street near the shambles, I am at rest at last." (453) Even in a state of rest, Mahood is a congeries of spheres, placed neatly in still another; his head, "covered with pustules and bluebottles," alone emerges from the jar; the rest of him, without thighs, legs, or feet (which have apparently just gangrened or rusted off) is an irregular loop within another (454). Within this roly-poly there exists a mind which is similarly spheroidically or spirally preoccupied with the questions and negations that are the novel's substance.

But then, The Unnamable is not strictly Mahood, nor is he any of the others; negation follows quickly on the heels of creation. His final naming is to be of Worm: "It will be my name too, when the time comes" (467). But he should like some evidence that he has existed, before he becomes Worm, "such as a kick in the arse, for example, or a kiss, the nature of the attention is of little importance, provided I cannot be suspected of being its author" (475). The desire is in the line—the last of the line—of the desires in Beckett's heroes to be recognized; one is reminded of Murphy's disquisition on the eternal Kick and the absence of the eternal Caress, though even a Kick from the great unknown is evidence of existence. But The Unnamable has succumbed to the "blooming buzzing confusion," the "spray of phenomena," and cannot discriminate among them, or himself from them.

In these terms, he can only spell out the rudiments of creation: "One alone, then others. One alone turned toward the all-impotent, all nescient, that haunts him, then others." (480) Is he the "one alone"? Has he created the others? It comes down to the absolute necessity for dying as an end-term of being born and living: If this is *not* a process of which you can be aware as participant and observer in one, "the thing stays where it is, nothing changes, within it, outside it, apparently, apparently." (514) The great scandal is not having any identity, and The Unnamable ends in a frenzy of disgust over this failure: "To have no identity, its a scandal, I assure you, look at this photograph, what, you see nothing, true for you, no matter, here, look at this death's head, you'll see, you'll be all right, it won't last long, here, look, here's the record, insults to policemen, indecent exposure, sins against holy ghost . . . etc." (523–24)

This and the passage that follows are an elaborate parody of official patterns of self-identification, of naming and numbering. The Unnamable, in not being able to answer any of the questions, testifies to his own anonymity and to the falsehoods of official procedure (rather like scenes in Kafka's *The Trial* and Ionesco's *The Killer*). The badges of identification, like the cunning of the Heideggerian "they" in Nathalie Sarraute's novels, are a cover for a vast anonymity and nondescriptness. What "they" want him to be isn't enough: "I must understand, I'm doing my best, I don't understand" (536). Strangely, but perhaps more surely than is at first apparent, The Unnamable concludes in an hysteria of can't and must and will. "I can't go on in any case. But I must go on. So I'll go on. Air, air, I'll seek air, air in time, the air of time, and in space, in my head, that's how I'll go on." (546)

The rhythms of contradiction and suasion continue to the end, which is not an end but a continuation, a process whose echoes ring in time and space. If he had some task, say to fill two vessels, or maybe four or a hundred, "to be emptied, the uneven to be filled, . . . in a certain way, a certain order." This is the "meaningful gesture," to correspond to the act of Emmett Kelly and his dustpan. There is the fable of the man "coming and going among his casks, trying to stop his hand from trembling, dropping his thimble, listening to it bouncing and rolling on the floor, scraping round for it with his foot, going down on his knees, going down on his belly, crawling" and so on: the man depending on the thimble which is himself or at least the act of himself. (554)

The novel and the trilogy end in that kind of ambiguous resolve, the comic-pathetic insistence on be-

ing as against the unbeing of E. E. Cummings' "mos-
tarians." "Where I am, I don't know, I'll never know,
in the silence you don't know, you must go on, I can't
go on, I'll go on" (577).

These hesitations, ambiguities, irresolutions are the
mess and mixture of existence and identity with
which the trilogy closes. With the exception of *Endgame*, where even the suggestion of them is rare indeed, and *Textes pour rien*, where almost everything
but the voices has disappeared, the theme continues
in the rest of Beckett's work. They are skillfully and
brilliantly dramatized as the acts of "Waiting" in his
most famous play.

THREE THINGS AT LEAST are important to the consideration of *Waiting for Godot*: its association with the traditions of the clown and with vaudeville, the question of Godot and his meaning, and the strategies of waiting. As for the first, we need to see it as an existentialist comedy, a genre not ordinarily associated with the philosophies of Sartre *et al.*, but in this case indispensably linked. It is a comedy in its many devices, taken from the reductive and derisive antics of the circus clown, and the vaudeville and the burlesque stage. It owes much to pantomime as well, of which Beckett has elsewhere proved himself a master. John R. Moore, in a wise essay on *Godot*, has suggested that we may consider "Gogo and Didi as very distant (perhaps the last) descendants of Don Quixote and Sancho Panza." [1] The parallel is justly indicated, but also shrewdly qualified. Estragon and Vladimir are very remote indeed from Don Quixote and Sancho Panza; they are not so much misguided idealist and comic realist, but both existential naturalists. Like the clown or comic, they are often naïve, patient, at times intensely practical and selfish, but durably patient. They exist in Murphy's world of the "nothing new," of continuously disappointed expectations.

There are many tricks which help to make *Godot* one of the greatest adaptations of the clown's skill to the theatre. One of these concerns the lines and curves of stage motion. The linear is indicated again and again by the device of repetition: Simple events, hopelessly trivial in themselves, in repetitive form become metaphysically fearsome. The major repetition is of course that of Act Two, which describes, with variations of some importance, the landscape, the characters, and the motions of Act One. This is to say that life will continue without much change, that expectations of change are generally disappointed, and that the line of time's descent to death is irreversible. The curve routines seem to run directly counter to the linear, as they do in Beckett's novels. But in the end they confirm, and even come to resemble, the linear, since they too are made up of repetitive motions. One of the direct effects of the curve in *Godot* is to destroy the notion of teleological purpose. Beckett's characters generally try to escape the straight line of mortality into the curve or sphere, but they are generally disillusioned. In accordance with time-honored suppositions, the curve is supposed to be more aesthetically pleasing as well as metaphysically impressive. But in *Godot* the "regard circulaire" has exactly the opposite effect. In vaudeville and burlesque routines, the cycle is used to define curves, the juggler keeps several spherical objects going in a circle, the spotlight describes a circle of space on the stage, where the comedian is on center. In *Godot*, however, curves are designed to describe the circular motion of human events; at best they are evasive, and postpone momentarily the line of movement toward mortality. In their most realistic aspect, they are simply forms of repetition—as in the "hat episode" of Act Two, or the "stuck whistle" stammerings of Lucky's "sermon." Most commonly effective is the suggestion of a curve as suggesting "resolution," or a progress of action in

drama. *Godot* defies this suggestion. Nothing is resolved in it; there are neither high points nor moments
of great passion; there are simply boredom and occasional relief from boredom.

The second comic routine in *Godot* is in the language itself. Beckett's language is "real" in the sense
of its being held to commonplace reality. Its realism is
indispensable to its critical function; his creatures are
victims both of a high degree of expectation spon-
sored by centuries of rational confidence and of their
own sobering recognitions of things as they miserably
are. The two languages—that of a metaphysically
stimulated confidence, that of an existential limitation—sometimes clash. Always, in *Godot*, the clash
is there, though it is often merely implicit. The impact
of situational realism is especially strong when it is defined within the limits of "tramps," hoboes, the
apotheosic "bum." Lawrence E. Harvey has usefully
summarized its effects: [2]

> He reduces our gourmet delicacies to carrots, black rad-
> ishes, and that staple of the starvation time under the
> German occupation, the lowly turnip. Our sex life leads
> to venereal disease; our fashionable clothes turn into
> rags, our lithe youth into stumbling old age, and our
> busy lives into a solitary waiting for death. We are not
> free but bound to each other and Godot; we are not
> equal but exist in a series of compartments in the social
> hierarchy; even our feelings of charity and fraternity are
> hesitant and fearful and inspired chiefly by our own
> selfish needs.

Illustrations of these uses of language are abundant;
two of them may be worth reproducing here; the first
combines disparagement of our delicate tastes and the
uncertainty of our relationship to authority:

ESTRAGON Give me a carrot. [*Vladimir rummages in
his pockets, takes out a turnip and gives it to Estra-*

gon who takes a bite out of it. Angrily.] It's a turnip!

VLADIMIR   Oh pardon! I could have sworn it was a carrot. [*He rummages again in his pockets, finds nothing but turnips.*] All that's turnips. [*He rummages.*] You must have eaten the last. [*He rummages.*] Wait, I have it. [*He brings out a carrot and gives it to Estragon.*] There, dear fellow. [*Estragon wipes the carrot on his sleeve and begins to eat it.*] Make it last, that's the end of them.

ESTRAGON   [*chewing*]. I asked you a question.

VLADIMIR   Ah.

ESTRAGON   Did you reply?

VLADIMIR   How's the carrot?

ESTRAGON   It's a carrot.

VLADIMIR   So much the better, so much the better. [*Pause.*] What was it you wanted to know?

ESTRAGON   I've forgotten. [*Chews.*] That's what annoys me. . . . Ah yes, now I remember.

VLADIMIR   Well?

ESTRAGON   [*his mouth full, vacuously*]. We're not tied?

VLADIMIR   I don't hear a word you're saying.

ESTRAGON   [*chews, swallows*]. I'm asking you if we're tied.

VLADIMIR   Tied?

ESTRAGON   Ti—ed.

VLADIMIR   How do you mean tied?

ESTRAGON   Down.

VLADIMIR   But to whom? By whom?

ESTRAGON   To your man.

VLADIMIR   To Godot? Tied to Godot! What an idea! No question of it. [*Pause.*] For the moment.

ESTRACON   His name is Godot?

VLADIMIR   I think so.

ESTRAGON   Fancy that. [*He raises what remains of the carrot by the stub of leaf, twirls it before his eyes.*] Funny, the more you eat the worse it gets.[3]

The second passage simply points up the confusion of arrangements, of timing, and in general of official calendars. It is akin to many uses of this satiric device, in the plays of Adamov, Genet, and especially Ionesco; in the last named, the cross-purposes technique has often reached the point of great comic drama. Here, Gogo and Didi discuss the time when they may expect Godot to arrive, but they are at a loss to determine the exact time *or* place.

VLADIMIR   A—. What are you insinuating? That we've come to the wrong place?

ESTRAGON   He should be here.

VLADIMIR   He didn't say for sure he'd come.

ESTRAGON   And if he doesn't come?

VLADIMIR   We'll come back to-morrow.

. . . .

ESTRAGON   You're sure it was this evening?

VLADIMIR   What?

ESTRAGON   That we were to wait.

VLADIMIR   He said Saturday. [*Pause.*] I think.

ESTRAGON   You think.

VLADIMIR   I must have made a note of it. [*He fumbles in his pockets, bursting with miscellaneous rubbish.*] [4]

ESTRAGON   [*very insidious*]. But what Saturday? And is it Saturday? Is it not rather Sunday? [*Pause.*] Or Monday? [*Pause.*] Or Friday?

VLADIMIR   [*looking wildly about him, as though the date was inscribed in the landscape*]. It's not possible!

ESTRAGON   Or Thursday?

VLADIMIR   What'll we do? [*10–10a*]

A third comic device of *Godot* is the pratfall, of which there are many variants. It is designed to express unwarranted or at least unexpected pain, and is often useful in the development of reductive satire. It is a comic destruction of cliché sentiments, and is therefore an important agent in maintaining the total effect of grim reality. The pratfall is any disgusting or vulgar defeat or collapse of sentimental expectations. When Estragon asks Vladimir to embrace him,

Vladimir obliges, but the effect is anything but sentimental: ". . . (Estragon recoils.) You stink of garlic!
Vladimir: It's for the kidneys. (Silence. Estragon
looks attentively at the tree.) What do we do now?
Estragon: Wait." (12) In another scene, when Estragon goes to comfort Lucky, who is weeping because
his master has spoken of killing him, he receives a kick
in the shins for his pains—this to destroy all pretense
of simple human sentiment:

> [*Estragon approaches Lucky and makes to wipe his
> eyes. Lucky kicks him violently in the shins. Estragon
> drops the handkerchief, recoils, staggers about the
> stage howling with pain.*] Hanky!
> [*Lucky puts down bag and basket, picks up handker-
> chief and gives it to Pozzo, goes back to his place,
> picks up bag and basket.*]
> ESTRAGON Oh the swine! [*He pulls up the leg of his
> trousers.*] He's crippled me!
> POZZO I told you he didn't like strangers. [21a–22]

The best example of deflation in *Godot* occurs in
Act Two. Pozzo has fallen, writhes, groans, beats the
ground with his fists, while Vladimir and Estragon try
to decide the wisdom of helping him. Perhaps we
ought first to take advantage of him, "subordinate our
good offices to certain conditions?" But Vladimir
urges that they help, because "It is not every day that
we are needed." (51) The two debate at cross purposes, while Pozzo groans for help. When they finally
agree, for two hundred francs, to the deed, Vladimir
falls too; then Estragon, trying to help him, stumbles
and falls. There follows a melee of fallen bodies and
violence, interspersed by cries for pity and charity.
(53–53a)

> ESTRAGON Suppose we got up to begin with?
> VLADIMIR No harm trying.
>   *They get up.*

ESTRAGON   Child's play.
VLADIMIR   Simple question of will-power.
ESTRAGON   And now?
POZZO   Help!
ESTRAGON   Let's go.
VLADIMIR   We can't.
ESTRAGON   Why not?
VLADIMIR   We're waiting for Godot. [54]

The comic routines are involved crucially in the play's development. Occasionally concerned with the larger questions of time and the prospects of eternity, they are otherwise devoted to the task of collapsing pretensions of any and all kinds. More than any others, they set the play's tone as abjectly low-tempered, with no high-flown rhetoric or hopes. The language and the contradictions, which follow quickly upon one another, serve to undercut all efforts to make the play's meaning somber or "significant" in any but the most strictly factual terms. *Godot* does not tolerate above-level sanctions or celebrations of the human state. And this reductive process applies as well to the Sartrean kind of dramatic emphasis. Edith Kern says [5] of Godot's existentialism: "But unlike Sartre, Beckett's characters are never 'en situation.' They are, rather, entirely removed from the more immediate problems of society and, not living within a social world, they do not play a part either in good faith or in bad. . . . They are never 'engagés,' or committed, never the god-like creators of their essence as men."

This point cannot be stressed enough; for, while *Godot* does address itself to some ideas and implies a view of many others, it is concerned above all with men without property and without authority. If it has any generalizing function, it is that the faculty for making generalities is invariably defective. For this reason, the dependence upon comic and burlesque routines is important. The circus clown, for example, often comes upon the scene just after a magnificent display of skill and grace; and, in the following routine (as a drunk trying the straight line, as a man who disgracefully fails in an elaborately planned demonstration of strength, or succeeds too easily), the clown brings the entire scene down to earth. Beyond this, there is no genuine metaphysical pathos in *Godot*. Estragon and Vladimir are erratically good-tempered and occasionally "helpful," but they have their price and are keenly aware of expedients. They are bumbling fools, but they are not "lovable rascals." In the general move toward the deflation of traditional values noticeable in the modern European theatre, *Godot* has a place. It is at times allied to Ionesco's extravagances (though not in any way to the reliance upon the political and moral assumptions of his *Rhinoceros*), and it occasionally reflects the manichaean topsy-turvy of Genet and Brecht. But few plays can equal it in skillful employment of the comic for a serious purpose; and nowhere else are the most significant and ponderous issues of our intellectual life so much reduced to scale.

ii

The first of these issues is the question of Godot himself. Who is he? And what does he "symbolize"? Estragon and Vladimir are "waiting for Godot," but they do not know who he is, nor when or even if he will come. Ronald Gray insists [6] that Godot *has* arrived, in the image of Pozzo perhaps but it may also be in a number of other manifestations, and that Gogo and Didi haven't recognized him. They are therefore "Christian delinquents," disbelievers, at the very least failing to understand God's manifold ways. This I think as far off the mark as criticism can be, the result of forcing external considerations upon the play.

Godot does not arrive, and he will not arrive. That he exists is at least established as a rumor, but his existence is not according to any theological explanation associated with divinity at all. He exists primarily in the minds and expectations of the two tramps, who therefore feel some necessity to honor an "agreement" to wait for him, according to a schedule dimly and confusedly understood. To Gogo and Didi, he must represent authority or power of some kind; he is not a rational or a consistent or even a likable figure, but he is presumably a man of power. He is "God" in this limited sense, but in any metaphysical sense God does not and cannot exist at all.

This fact is satisfactorily evidenced in the play, and evidence for it of a kind can be found in Beckett's fiction: No Beckett character is seriously interested in God as a metaphysical entity; He is too remote to excite them, and in any case they are almost invariably thrown back on their own resources of imagination and reason for self-definition. Godot is no more God than is the Mr. Knott whom Watt serves. The suggestions of a remote theological being fail to attract the inhabitants of Beckett's world, who choose the metaphors and techniques of transcendence that are to their own liking. As Beckett says of Joyce's, so he might have said of his own work: that his is a world of "vegetation," where people wait, or endure existence, without great expectations beyond mortality. The Christian beliefs are turned to secular metaphors; and the great line of progress in time is toward death rather than either a secular or a theological perfection.

This is not to say that Gogo and Didi are not interested in theological questions. They show on several occasions a lively interest in incidental religious exegesis. In the beginning, the question is raised of the two thieves crucified on either side of Jesus; this is a scene Beckett has explored before, in *The Unnamable*, and in a drastically revisionist style. In *Godot*, Didi brings up the matter: only one of the thieves was supposed to have been saved. Saved from what, asks Gogo; from Hell, says Didi. How is it, he continues, that "of the four Evangelists only one speaks of a thief being saved. The four of them were there—or thereabouts—and only one of them speaks of a thief being saved." (9) But in the ensuing dialogue, it turns out that Didi is not interested in salvation from hell, but only from death. And the theological interests of both are generally limited to life, death, and pain. At another time, Gogo is removing his boots and Didi says, "But you can't go barefoot!"

ESTRAGON   Christ did.
VLADIMIR   Christ! What has Christ got to do with it? You're not going to compare yourself to Christ!
ESTRAGON   All my life I've compared myself to him.
VLADIMIR   But where he lived it was warm, it was dry!
ESTRAGON   Yes. And they crucified quick.
       Silence. [34a]

In both of these cases, the interest in religion is extremely personal. In the first, it is the matter of justice that interests them, and justice not for Christ but for the thieves; that, and the reliability of evidence interests them. Biblical literature is always so reduced in Beckett's work. There are no heroics, and theological disputation—so interesting and vital to Joyce's Stephen Dedalus—is as effectively deflated as are metaphysical and rational suppositions. The most striking case of this deflationary process is Lucky's "sermon," more properly his "talk," which is viewed as an entertainment in lieu of the dancing Pozzo would prefer to have him do. Lucky's speech has to do with all pretenses common to an "age of progress," the end-result of two and a half centuries of rational confidence. In his *PMLA* article (*p. 139*), Lawrence Harvey has said of him that, "when he begins to think, he not only deflates the intellectual but at the same time satirizes into non-existence our many specialized professional and avocational categories." [7]

At the urging of Pozzo to "Think!" which is a kind of injected stimulus, Lucky begins, on the question of God's existence: "Given the existence as uttered forth in the public works of Puncher and Wattmann of a personal God . . ." The speech is interrupted by a "quid pro quaqua quaqua" which has the sound of "quack" and in its repetition is a deflationary device. ". . . with white beard quaquaquaqua outside time without extension who from the heights of divine apathia divine athambia divine aphasia loves us dearly with some exceptions for reasons unknown . . ." (*28a*) His fumbling for words is dramatically suitable, but also a parody of the theological "naming" of concepts. Lucky's qualifications of the truth are also a far-ranging abuse of theological squeamishness; and he proceeds, to indicate in his stammer further unwitting irreverence for the "Acacacacademy of Anthropopopometry of Essy-in-Possy," which establishes "beyond all doubt all other doubt than that which clings to the labors of men, . . ." establishes exactly nothing, since other commentaries have hopelessly confused the desire for proof. The tirade proceeds, to a parody of the defects of "applied sciences": ". . . the strides of alimentation and defecation wastes and pines wastes and pines and concurrently simultaneously what is more for reasons unknown in spite of the strides of physical culture the practice of sports such as tennis football running cycling swimming fly-

ing floating riding gliding conating camogie . . ."
and so on. The parody continues, of the view that
salvation can be measured exactly in terms of the
utilitarian rule: ". . . approximately by and large
more or less to the nearest decimal good measure
round figures stark naked in the stockinged felt in
Connemara . . ." (28a–29). The prevailing and re-
current phrase is "for reasons unknown," there being
so many more reasons unknown than reasons known
for confidence in rationalist commentaries.

God cannot survive such claptrap, and He does not
survive. All theological questions must therefore be
brought down to the quizzical personal doubts and
definitions of Gogo and Didi. The question whether
Godot *is* God or "equals God" should apparently be
answered. God is surely one of the integers in Beckett's calculus. The Christian view of God, or definition of Him, is so much a part of moral discussion
that any treatment of the human condition within
that tradition must account for it. This is very different, however, from making it directly a part of the
speculations of Gogo and Didi. One critic considered
Godot an "orthodox" Christian work: "The tramps
with their rags and their misery represent the fallen
state of man. The squalor of their surroundings, their
lack of a 'stake in the world,' represents the idea that
here in this world we can build no abiding city. The
ambiguity of their attitude towards Godot, their
mingled hope and fear, the doubtful tone of the boy's
messages, represent the state of tension and uncertainty in which the average Christian must live in this
world, avoiding presumption and also avoiding despair." [8] This is surely a narrow and a "wishful" interpretation. *Godot* does not argue an orthodox Christian
view of doubt and despair; in fact, the doubt and de-

spair are a consequence of the strong reasons for dismissing a personal God who is responsible for a system of moral sanctions and rewards.

Much energy has been spent on the meaning of the word, Godot; it is given in other forms in the play: "Godet," "Godin"; Gogo and Didi are not sure that Pozzo isn't Godot, and Pozzo himself confuses the name in several ways.[9] There is no question that Godot is an eternal "father image," an image of authority deeply wished for and so controlling the imaginations of the two tramps that they consider "waiting for him" a major preoccupation and duty. But the *reliance* upon the existence of an eternal being, to the neglect of personal responsibility for existence, is a major object of Beckett's criticism. The view of Godot is nontheological and untraditional; it is a form of anthropomorphic relationship, if you wish. But *Waiting for Godot* is an existentialist play, and as such it argues against the assumption of an image that drains off the energy of stark human responsibility. If Beckett may be said to be directly criticizing forms of supernatural presumption, it is in terms of the vitiating effects of such diversions of energy. In fact, "waiting" is in itself a meaningless activity, if it is a waiting for a specific supporting force. The two tramps describe again and again the futility of such expectations.

iii

Near the play's end, Vladimir puts the question of "waiting" quite frankly and eloquently. Waiting equals existing within a time scheme that permits none of the comforts of eternity.

[*Estragon, having struggled with his boots in vain, is dozing off again. Vladimir looks at him.*] He'll know nothing. He'll tell me about the blows he received and

I'll give him a carrot. [*Pause.*] Astride of a grave and a difficult birth. Down in the hole lingeringly, the grave-digger puts on the forceps. We have time to grow old. The air is full of our cries. [*He listens.*] But habit is a great deadener. [*He looks again at Estragon.*] At me too someone is looking, of me too someone is saying, He is sleeping, he knows nothing, let him sleep on. [*Pause.*] I can't go on! [*Pause.*] What have I said? [58–58a]

Waiting is the crucial experience of the Beckett character. It involves enduring the world's nonsense, its absurdity, without clear hope of immediate or direct help. The world is charged with mortality: the grave-digger applies the forceps, Death succeeds to life, which succeeds to death. Act Two succeeds Act One as irrevocably and monotonously as Gogo and Didi can predict each other's gestures and eccentricities. In his essay on Proust, Beckett had spoken about the relationship of habit and the act of "suffering" time. Vladimir says, "Habit is a great deadener." The landscape of *Godot* is monotonous and barren. The two tramps are forever asking "What shall we do now?" or seeking diversion. When Pozzo and Lucky leave the first time, the shouting and the crying gone once again, Vladimir says: "That passed the time."

ESTRAGON It would have passed in any case.
VLADIMIR Yes, but not so rapidly.
        Pause.
ESTRAGON What do we do now?
VLADIMIR I don't know.
ESTRAGON Let's go.
VLADIMIR We can't.
ESTRAGON Why not?
VLADIMIR We're waiting for Godot. [31a]

The situation of *Godot* is a dreadful void, an emptiness, a wearisome threat of boredom, a desperate need to "fill in the holes of time." The time, moreover, proceeds in a straight line toward death. The directions for Act Two are starkly relevant: Next day. Same time. Same place. The motifs of repetition seal the dreary fate. The round song of the dog in the kitchen is available for endless repetition, and it serves Vladimir to fill in a dread space of loneliness until Estragon arrives on the second day. (37–37*a*) Vladimir spies Lucky's hat, left there from the day before, and then begins a circular hat motion: "Estragon takes Vladimir's hat. Vladimir adjusts Lucky's hat on his head. Estragon puts on Vladimir's hat in place of his own which he hands to Vladimir. Vladimir takes Estragon's hat." (46) And so on. It is an example of the variants and combinations and systems we discover in *Watt* and *Molloy*.

Along with the monotony of "waiting," there is the inevitability of the line moving toward age and death, that "fearful descending line that ends in the grave," as Lawrence Harvey describes it (*PMLA*, 141). The characters change in the time span of the play; they grow weaker. Lucky, who used to dance for Pozzo's entertainment, now can only "think" and talk. (In Act Two he has become mute.) As the play progresses, persons have increasing difficulty in standing up, sustaining themselves. Habit and familiarity grow increasingly boring and irksome.

Waiting has only two possible reliefs and justifications: that it is "for Godot"; that it may either be borne or stopped. Suicide is possible, within the range of human choice. But no one commits suicide; the limb of the tree, for one thing, is too frail, and it would break. In any case, neither Gogo nor Didi has the "strength" to initiate a suicide attempt. Waiting is not susceptible of melodramatic gestures. It is a solemn and a dreadful obligation, and nowhere is that fact more poignantly stated than in the passage at the beginning of Act Two (quoted above). Here, it is the succession of expected events that forms the heart of the experience.

Like all other Beckett characters, Gogo and Didi must not only "fill time" but assert and prove existence, ally themselves forcefully with other existing beings. The dangers of nonexistence forever threaten, and they are even a temptation. *Waiting for Godot*, says Jean Jacques Mayoux, "is on one level a dialectic of suicide, for to wait is to live. Suicide thus appears as a rational decision which should have been undertaken after the very first awareness of the absurdity of life. Once caught up in the 'waiting,' however, no instant of time can ever be decisive again." [10] Waiting is therefore a condition of man; it involves an acceptance both of death and of life.

iv

Beckett's other plays are extensions of *Waiting for Godot*. If anything, *Endgame* carries the reductive process even further. The setting reminds us of the spatial limits of *Malone Dies* and *The Unnamable*: it is a room with two small windows high up and no accessible view. "Bare interior." "Grey light." In the center Hamm sits in a wheel chair, a blood-stained handkerchief over his no-face. Clov pronounces on the ineluctable progress of death: "Finished, it's finished, nearly finished, it must be nearly finished. (Pause.) Grain upon grain, one by one, and one day, suddenly, there's a heap, a little heap, the impossible heap." [11]

The only diversion is for Clov to take Hamm for a "trip around the world," or for him to climb to the window, to see if the world actually exists. Turning about the room in his wheel chair, Hamm is sure that he must be "right in the center." Also in the geometrical economy of the situation is the wall, which Hamm touches with his hand: "Beyond is the . . . other hell." (*p. 26*) At Hamm's request, Clov looks out the window through his telescope:

> Let's see.
> [*He looks, moving the telescope.*]
> Zero . . .
>
> . . . .
> HAMM   Nothing stirs. All is—
>
> . . . .
> CLOV   Corpsed.
>   [*Pause.*]
>   Well? Content?
> HAMM   Look at the sea.
> CLOV   It's the same.
> HAMM   Look at the ocean! [29–30]

Endgame is a step removed from *Waiting for Godot*, toward death. Both Clov and Hamm await death, and, it would seem, the end of the world. In an outburst of death's-edge rhetoric, Hamm shouts out: "Use your head, can't you, use your head, you're on earth, there's no cure for that!" (68) And, a few lines later, begs himself to hold on a little longer: ". . . the stillness. If I can hold my piece, and sit quiet, it will be all over with sound, and motion, all over and done with" (69). He goes the whole way, to his death: "Moments for nothing, now as always, time was never and time is over, reckoning closed and story ended" (83). There is something curiously static about *Endgame*; it is in Thomas Barbour's view "not so much a short play as a very long metaphysical poem." [12] This impression is a natural consequence of the limitations of the play's movement. It is neither so varied nor so embellished as *Godot*. Nor is it so rich as the novels; the simply stated formulas of *Endgame* are in the novels elaborately spun out, and here on the stage they can offer only a limited development. But the very limitation is in some respects an advantage. Clov and Hamm describe the arc of a diminished human pretension. They are at the end of life, perhaps near the end of the world. Outside, in "that other hell," there seems no sign of animation; and the father and mother images have disappeared, each in its trash can, no longer to force their lids.

The great difference between the novels and the plays is that the torrent of words diminishes, and in fact—as Beckett's more recent plays testify—may cease altogether. As the words slow down, gesture, look, the simple moves of the body take over. A form of miming has its own poetic effect, and conveys— perhaps in a less complicated way—its own meaning. *Endgame* is less dependent on words than *Waiting for Godot*; it is also less an elaboration of the themes both plays share. "Acts without Words: I" relies upon stage spaces and props, distances and a limited number of actions. Its comedy simplifies the essential idea. The man at center is thrown onto the stage, gets up, dusts himself off, reflects, goes out again, is flung back. Objects are lowered from the flies, offered to him, withdrawn again. Each time he suffers a rebuke, he pauses to reflect, fastidiously attends to his hands, rises to try again. Eventually, he does not move, but simply allows temptations to go unnoticed. He has learned to depend only upon himself, as Barbour says, to "count on nothing but the unvarnished fact of his existence."

Krapp's Last Tape may be said to have two voices— or, rather, one actor who mimes and the tape record of his voice. Again, the themes so elaborated in the novels are here drastically simplified. One may say that they are extracted from the novels, made over for visual representation, and suffer in the transition and immense simplification. Yet this is a form to which Beckett's talent is remarkably suited. Krapp is a perfect specimen of the Beckettian man, reduced in powers of expression to gestures and postures. He is the clown turned meditative. His situation is as desperate as those of Gogo and Didi, and like them he has perceptibly aged. The skull grins beneath the flesh. But there are few details, few props, fewer ideas. He is, in short, in the act of reviewing his past, and he uses a tape-recorder to recapture it.

The description of his few simple actions shows a masterful skill in silent techniques. "He stoops, unlocks first drawer, peers into it, feels about inside it, takes out a reel of tape, peers at it, puts it back, locks drawer, unlocks second drawer, peers into it, feels about inside it, takes out a large banana, peers at it, locks drawer, puts keys back in his pocket. He turns, advances to edge of stage, halts, strokes banana, peels it, drops skin at his feet, puts end of banana in his mouth and remains motionless, staring vacuously before him." [13]

The materials are all here borrowed from the tradition of the clown and the pantomimist. The words are a comic version of A la recherche du temps perdu. The tape recorder stutters out a few family-album fragments, to which Krapp attends with the aid of legend and dictionary. "Slight improvement in bowel condition . . . Hm . . . Memorable . . . what? (He peers closer.) Equinox, memorable equinox. (He raises his head, stares blankly front. Puzzled.) Memorable equinox? . . . (Pause. He shrugs his shoulders, peers again at ledger, reads.) Farewell to— (he turns the page) —love." (p. 13)

The "last tape" presents him to himself as thirty-nine (a voice "clearly Krapp's at a much earlier time"): ". . . sound as a bell, apart from my old

weakness, and intellectually I have now every reason
to suspect at the . . . (hesitates) . . . crest of the
wave—or thereabouts." (14) Krapp "participates in"
the life of the tape, laughs appreciatively with it,
puzzles occasionally over lost meanings and obscure
allusions. "Closing with a— (brief laugh) —yelp to
Providence. (Prolonged laugh in which Krapp
joins.)" (17) But he becomes impatient with the
tape's garrulity, winds it forward to the moment he
wants to hear: "—my face in her breasts and my
hand on her. We lay there without moving. But under
us all moved, and moved us, gently, up and down, and
from side to side." (21) Krapp has obviously reached
the past moment he wants to relive, winds the tape
back so that it may be repeated (22–23). After a few
drinks off-stage, he comes back, and to a new running
of the recorder denounces "That stupid bastard I took
myself for thirty years ago" (24). But in the act of
denunciation of that "crud," the thirty-year-old memory sticks; and at last he adjusts the tape so that it will
repeat it (27). As the tape concludes, the voice says,
"But I wouldn't want them back. Not with the fire
in me now. No, I wouldn't want them back./Krapp
motionless staring before him. The tape runs on in
silence," as the curtain descends. (28)

This is a simplified Proustian exercise, or better a
parody of Proust. It is loaded with the sentimentality
of the old man caught in a moment of his past, his
present a fumbling remnant of it. But even this overly
simple rendering of Beckett's conceptions testifies to
his skill in using the language of the self.

Some idea of his views of the self may be captured
from it; but, more so, from the plays taken together.
Their major assumption is that of existential time
leading inevitably toward death. Within its passing,
there are boredom and desperate strategies to give it

significance, or simply to "pass the time." Pozzo, momentarily infuriated by Didi's questions, gives the clue to this blank perspective upon experience: "One day, is that not enough for you, one day he went dumb, one day I went blind, one day we'll go deaf, one day we were born, one day we shall die, the same day, the same second, is that not enough for you? (Calmer.) They give birth astride of a grave, the light gleams an instant, then it's night once more." (*Godot*, 57*a*)

Within this span of time—this lifetime, this day, this second—the Beckett hero is beset by boredom and pain. Unlike his narrative characters, the heroes of his plays have a limited repertory of devices, whether for passing the time or or stopping it. They weave in and out of existence, at once puzzling over its tedium and depressed with their failure to define their actions significantly. When a sentimental note is briefly struck—as in *All That Fall* and *Embers*, two radio plays—it is entertained ironically. The Beckett hero is self-sufficient only when he is starkly alone, has been disabused by the vitality of the Godot image, has brought the world to his level, and is asked uncompromisingly to endure it for what it is. In the plays, the machinery of rationality, the ingenious extensions of consciousness and prolongings of innocence of the novels, are reduced to a minimum. The "man-using-machine" image so prominent in *Molloy* and other fictions is only fitfully and ironically seen; in *Krapp's Last Tape* the machine is a mechanical "memory" to which he addresses his attention. It does nothing to complement what he is, but fixes a part of what he was in his consciousness.

This is the starkest, blankest kind of existential world. The Beckett man is neither existentially curious nor heroically *engagé*. Over all of his meditations there is the awful prospect that (*a*) he can depend only on the world of phenomena (*Godot*) and (*b*) the world of phenomena seems to be disappearing (*Endgame*). In these circumstances, it is difficult to suppose a "Godot" as a god of any kind; he may be a business man or a Cabinet Minister or a Werner von Braun; he is not God.

The alternative choices are extremely limited. As in the novels, they consist of a frantic succession of can't, must, will. To "go on" is to persist in being one's doubting self. The rhetoric of recent works seems to have accelerated the hysteria of *The Unnamable*. In her *Perspective* article (*pp.* 127–28), Ruby Cohn reports Beckett as having said that "*The Unnamable* drove him into an impasse from which his *Textes pour rien* could not extricate him." The *Textes* bear testimony of this impasse; they become, as Miss Cohn says, "epistemological poetry." The "I" is no longer so much concerned with the relationships of selves as with the rhetoric of basic uncertainties. "Est-ce possible [he says in *Texte XIII*], est-ce là enfin la chose possible, que s'éteigne ce noir rien aux ombres impossibles, là enfin la chose faisable, que l'infaisable finisse et se taise le silence, elle se le demande, cette voix qui est silence, ou moi, comment savoir, de mon moi de trois lettres, ce sont là des songes, des silences qui se valent, elle et moi, elle et lui, moi et lui, et tous les nôtres." [14]

v

Beckett's work brings the "language of the self" to an inescapable impasse. The lines of descent to which it belongs have been described in chapters one through three above. They are chiefly in the Western rational, skeptical tradition beginning with the speculative opportunities offered by Descartes' dualism.

Beckett simply takes the self as a starting point, sub-ordinates all of the vast and systematic orders of meta-physical explanation to the position of a cluster of metaphors available to the inquiring self, and pro-ceeds then to a narrative and dramatic series of medi-tations upon them.

The other line of descent, fully given in chapter one above, is important not so much for its having shifted the ground of observation to the self as for its having reduced its prepossessiveness—the elements of human dignity—within it. The self is not only a skeptical in-quirer in this case, but emotionally dispossessed and depressed. It is an important factor in this literature that the "tragic vision" becomes more and more a per-sonal vision, or a nightmare of introspection.

Both the Russian-to-Kafka metaphors and the Des-cartes-to-Joyce techniques are significantly relevant to a full view of Beckett's world. The Kafka hero is al-ways in danger of becoming vermin, animal, of dying "like a dog" or living like a cockroach; the rationales of respectability risk constantly a deterioration of confidence; and the rhetoric, magnificently though deceptively "realistic," is accelerated in conditions where the self's boundaries are invaded. Dostoevsky's undergroundling always speculates on three levels: that of himself, that of the mirror image of himself (which throws back the self, though with significant refractions), that of the logical equations of reason. All of these are taken up in Beckett, though the third comes natively to him through Descartes and the ra-tionalistic orders of meditation.

Beckett's selves are, to begin with, persons without God, or (Murphy and Watt) persons with God im-perfectly within them. As they proceed (chiefly from novel to play to comic interlude or sketch), their deliberations are fixed upon the fragments both of a rational order and of a once well established and defended *amour-propre*. As confidence in either systematic order or self declines, the rhetoric becomes disengaged, runs off on its own. Only in the plays does the result come within perceptible scope and order: and this because the requirements of the theatre, however ignored or adapted to his tastes, do make for a more than occasional comprehension of Beckett's dispositions. Yet the theatre also oversimplifies; and, as the *Textes pour rien* prove, the "pure rhetoric" of Beckett's "residual Cartesian" is limited and impeded by dramatic necessities.

The essential "doctrine" of Beckett's work is nevertheless contained within his best play (and one of the best of all contemporary plays), *Waiting for Godot*. It is that life consists of "waiting," an individually existential premise which incites no one to an exercise of a Sartrean "dreadful freedom" but has its own agonies and dreads. It is an agony to "wait for Godot" in a place deprived of almost all recognizable natural promise and from a point-of-view all but deprived of confidence. But we "can't go on, we must go on, we will go on": unquestioning, as the Unnamable says, but also unbelieving, in "It, say it, not knowing what" (*Three Novels* 401).

NOTES

Chapter 1

1. In *The Best Short Stories of Dostoevsky*, trans. David Magarshack (New York: Modern Library, 1959).

2. In *The Portable Russian Reader*, trans. Bernard Guilbert Guerney (New York: Viking, 1947), p. 58.

3. In *The Overcoat and Other Stories*, trans. Constance Garnett (New York: Knopf, 1923), p. 134.

4. *Oblomov*, trans. David Magarshack (Harmondsworth, England: Penguin Books, 1954).

5. Rufus Mathewson, *The Positive Hero in Soviet Literature* (New York: Columbia University Press, 1958), p. 47.

6. Quoted by David Magarshack, *Turgenev* (London: Faber and Faber, 1954), p. 99.

7. *Ibid.*, p. 198. See also Joseph Frank, "Nihilism and *Notes from the Underground*," *Sewanee Review* (Winter 1961), pp. 1–33. Mr. Frank claims that Dostoevsky's book was intended primarily as a parody of Chernyshevski's position.

8. Translated by George Reavey (New York: Noonday, 1958). Turgenev's title was *Fathers and Children*, but it always seems to come out *Sons* in translation.

9. Translated by Constance Garnett (New York: Macmillan, 1917).

10. *The Devils*, trans. David Magarshack (Harmondsworth, England: Penguin Books, 1953), pp. 614–15.

11. Even in *Notes from the Underground*, from which the references to Christ were excised by the censor, Lisa is of the type of Raskolnikov's Sonia.

12. See Ralph Matlaw, "Structure and Integration in

Notes from the Underground," PMLA, 73 (Mar. 1958), 101–9.

13. The lodgings of the underground man are not of course *in* the underground; they are one of several "basements" in a drab house.

14. *The Brothers Karamazov,* trans. David Magarshack (Harmondsworth: Penguin Books, 1958), I, 298.

15. Quoted by David Magarshack in the Introduction to his translation of *The Idiot* (Harmondsworth: Penguin Books, 1955), p. 7.

16. When his reading is finished, Terentyev dramatically offers his suicide, which fails to come off. This scene is a parody of all staged suicides in Russian literature.

17. *Dostoevsky's Underground Man in Russian Literature* (The Hague: Mouton, 1958).

18. In *The Penal Colony,* trans. Willa and Edwin Muir (New York: Schocken Books, 1948).

19. "A Hunger-Artist," in *Franz Kafka Today* (Madison: University of Wisconsin Press, 1958), pp. 61–70.

20. *The Penal Colony,* p. 248.

21. In *Three Novels,* trans. by Patrick Bowles and the author (New York: Grove Press, 1959).

22. *Malone Dies,* in *Three Novels,* p. 304.

23. Translated by the author (New York: Grove Press, 1958).

24. *Proust* (New York: Grove Press, 1957), pp. 4–5.

25. *Waiting for Godot,* trans. by author (New York: Grove Press, 1954), p. 34.

Chapter 2

1. "Point of View in Modern Fiction . . . ," PMLA, 70 (Dec. 1955), 1162.

2. *L'Ère du Soupçon* (Paris: Gallimard, 1956). This quotation is from the book's title essay, trans. Maria Jolas, which was published separately in *Noonday,* 1 (1958), 94.

3. *Perspective,* 11 (Autumn 1959), 134.

4. Ralph M. Eaton's Introduction to Descartes' *Selections* (New York: Scribner's, 1927), p. xxiv.

5. Albert G. A. Balz, *Descartes and the Modern Mind* (New Haven: Yale University Press, 1952), p. 174.

6. Virginia Woolf, *To the Lighthouse* (New York: Harcourt, Brace, 1927), p. 158.

7. Henry James, *The Ambassadors* (New York: Rinehart Editions, 1960), p. 142. First published 1903.

8. Respectively, Henry James, *The Portrait of a Lady* (Boston: Houghton, Mifflin, 1956; first published, 1881), p. 451, and James Joyce, *Ulysses* (New York: Random House, 1934), p. 39.

9. Preface to *Portrait of a Man Unknown*, trans. Maria Jolas (New York: George Braziller, 1958), p. xii.

10. *Our Exagmination Round His Factification for Incamination of Work in Progress* (London: Faber and Faber, n.d.), pp. 21–22. First published 1929.

11. *A Portrait of the Artist as a Young Man* (New York: Compass Books, 1956), p. 90.

12. "*Things* in Recent French Literature," *PMLA*, 71 (Mar. 1956), 27.

13. They are often similar to Lucky's speech in Part One of *Waiting for Godot*; see Chapter 5 below.

14. Translated by Donald M. Allen in *Four Plays* (New York: Grove Press, 1958), pp. 158–60.

15. Alain Robbe-Grillet, "A Fresh Start for Fiction," trans. Richard Howard, *Evergreen Review*, 3 (1957), 100.

16. *Saint-Genet: Comédien et Martyr* (Paris: Gallimard, 1952), p. 12.

17. "The Theatre of the Absurd," *Tulane Drama Review*, 4 (Summer 1960), 5.

Chapter 3

1. *Whoroscope* (Paris: The Hours Press, 1958), lines 60–65.

2. "The Beckett Landscape," *Spectrum*, 2 (Winter 1958), 8.

3. *The Killer and Other Plays*, trans. Donald Watson (New York: Grove Press, 1960), p. 93.

4. *Ceremony and Other Poems* (New York: Harcourt, Brace, 1950), p. 18.

5. "The Clowns," in *Selected Writings of Jules Laforgue*, trans. William Jay Smith (New York: Grove Press, 1956), p. 45. The original "Les Pierrots" is in *Oeuvres*, I, 221.

6. *The Great God Pan* (New York: Hermitage House, 1952), p. 8.

7. "Text for Nothing I," trans. by the author, *Evergreen Review*, 9 (Summer 1959), 21.

8. In *Krapp's Last Tape and Other Dramatic Pieces*, trans. by the author (New York: Grove Press, 1960), pp. 125, 129.

9. *Out of This Century* (New York: Dial, 1946), pp. 194–97.

10. See above, Chapter 1. Miss Guggenheim says that "I made him read the book and of course he immediately saw the resemblance between himself and the strange inactive hero who finally did not even have the will-power to get out of bed."

11. Richard Ellmann speaks of Beckett reading aloud to Joyce (in 1932) from Mauthner's *Beiträge zu Einer Kritik der Sprache*, "in which the nominalistic view of language seemed something Joyce was looking for." *James Joyce* (New York: Oxford University Press, 1959), pp. 661–62.

12. In *Evergreen Review*, 1 (1957), 192.

13. Ruby Cohn, "Preliminary Observations," *Perspective*, 11 (Autumn 1959), 121.

14. *Dante's Drama of the Mind* (Princeton: Princeton University Press, 1953), p. 15.

15. Translated by Dorothy Sayers (Harmondsworth: The Penguin Classics, 1955), p. 98.

16. "Dante's Belacqua and Beckett's Tramps," *Comparative Literature*, 11 (Summer 1959), 259.

17. *Murphy* (New York: Grove Press, 1957), p. 78.

18. *More Pricks Than Kicks* (London: Chatto and Windus, 1934), p. 43.

Chapter 4

1. *"Watt," Perspective*, 11 (Autumn 1959), 167.

2. "Samuel Beckett and the Anti-Novel," *London Magazine*, 5 (Dec. 1958), 41–42.

3. *Watt* (New York: Grove Press, 1959), p. 25.

4. Ruby Cohn, article cited, *Perspective*, 11 (Autumn 1959), 123.

5. *Molloy* in *Three Novels*, pp. 3, 4, 7–9.

6. In this connection, it is significant that Molloy's town is called Watt (100).

7. The thought of suicide occurs to Molloy, as it does to other Beckett characters, but he sets it aside. "The idea of strangulation in particular, however tempting, I always overcame, after a short struggle." (103–4)

8. "Moran-Molloy: The Hero as Author," *Perspective*, 11 (Autumn 1959), 185.

9. *Malone Dies* in *Three Novels*, p. 243.

10. *The Unnamable* in *Three Novels*, p. 401.

11. "The Mathematical Limit," *Nation*, 188 (Feb. 14, 1959), 145.

Chapter 5

1. "A Farewell to Something," *Tulane Drama Review*, 5 (Sept. 1960), 59.

2. "Art and the Existential in *En Attendant Godot*," *PMLA*, 75 (Mar. 1960), 139.

3. *Waiting for Godot*, pp. 14–14a. For some reason, the Evergreen edition numbered only alternate pages. The "a" references are therefore to the pages facing those numbered.

4. Cf. the incident of Edouard's brief case in Act Two of Ionesco's *The Killer*.

5. "Drama Stripped for Inaction: Beckett's *Godot*," *Yale French Studies*, no. 14 (Winter 1954–55), 47.

6. " 'Waiting for Godot': A Christian Interpretation," *The Listener*, 57 (Jan. 24, 1957), 160–61.

7. The closest link of Beckett to Ionesco is in this "speech." Ionesco has many times lampooned similar pre-

tensions. In *Amédée*, the hero disappears skyward, shouting progressive inanities; Bérenger of *The Killer* is a stickler for the word and ideal of progress, "un possibiliste avant la lettre"; he becomes the "hero" of *Rhinoceros* and thus may be said to have "saved" Ionesco from liberal critics. Pompous and naïve conventions are of course satirized often in Ionesco's plays: *The Chairs*, where the "dearly beloved" old man fulfills his promise of a vital message in the word ANGELFOOD written on the blackboard by a deaf-mute "orator"; the notorious *Bald Soprano*, where the favorite clichés run afoul of absurd cross-purposes; the family scene of *Jack, or the Submission*, etc.

8. *Times Literary Supplement*, Feb. 10, 1956, p. 84.

9. In his *Perspective* article (p. 136), Hugh Kenner even finds a Godeau, a French cyclist, whose skill links him with Descartes.

10. "The Theatre of Samuel Beckett," *Perspective*, 11 (Autumn 1959), 151.

11. *Endgame*, trans. by the author (New York: Grove Press, 1958), p. 1.

12. "Beckett and Ionesco," *Hudson Review*, 11 (Summer 1958), 272.

13. *Krapp's Last Tape* (New York: Grove Press, 1960), pp. 10–11.

14. *Nouvelles et textes pour rien* (Paris: Les Editions de Minuit, 1955), pp. 218–19.

BIBLIOGRAPHY

PRIMARY WORKS CITED

Beckett, Samuel. "Echo's Bones," *Evergreen Review*, no. 1 (1957), 179–92.

———. *Endgame*. Translated by the author. New York: Grove Press, 1958.

———. *Krapp's Last Tape and Other Dramatic Pieces*. Translated by the author. New York: Grove Press, 1960.

———. *Molloy, Malone Dies* and *The Unnamable, Three Novels*. Translated by Patrick Bowles and the author. New York: Grove Press, 1959.

———. *More Pricks Than Kicks*. London: Chatto and Windus, 1934.

———. *Murphy*. New York: Grove Press, 1957.

———. *Our Exagmination Round His Factification for Incamination of Work in Progress*. London: Faber and Faber, 1929.

———. *Proust*. New York: Grove Press, 1957.

———. *Waiting for Godot*. Translated by the author. New York: Grove Press, 1954.

———. *Watt*. New York: Grove Press, 1959.

———. *Whoroscope*. Paris: The Hours Press, 1958.

Dostoevsky, Fedor. *The Brothers Karamazov*. Translated by David Magarshack. Harmondsworth, England: Penguin Books, 1958.

———. *The Devils*. Translated by David Magarshack. Harmondsworth: Penguin Books, 1953.

———. *The Idiot*. Translated by David Magarshack. Harmondsworth: Penguin Books, 1955.

———. *Notes from the Underground* in *The Best Short Stories of Dostoevsky*. Translated by David Magarshack. New York: Modern Library, 1959.

Gogol, Nikolai V. "A Madman's Diary," in *The Overcoat and Other Stories*. Translated by Constance Garnett. New York: Knopf, 1923.

———. "The Overcoat," in *The Portable Russian Reader*. Translated by Bernard Guilbert Guerney. New York: Viking, 1947.

Goncharov, Ivan A. *Oblomov*. Translated by David Magarshack. Harmondsworth: Penguin Books, 1954.

Joyce, James. *Ulysses*. New York: Random House, 1934.

Kafka, Franz. "Metamorphosis" and "A Hunger Artist" in *The Penal Colony*. Translated by Willa and Edwin Muir. New York: Schocken Books, 1948.

Turgenev, Ivan S. *Fathers and Sons*. Translated by George Reavey. New York: Noonday, 1958.

———. *Virgin Soil*. Translated by Constance Garnett. New York: Macmillan, 1917.

SELECTED BECKETT CRITICISM

[This list includes only items cited or especially helpful in the preparation of this book. Essays of exceptional value are marked with an asterisk. There are at present no other books on the subject, though books have been projected by Hugh Kenner, Mrs. Ruby Cohn, and Melvin Friedman. For a more complete checklist see *Perspective*, 11 (Autumn 1959), 193–96.]

Barbour, Thomas. "Beckett and Ionesco," *Hudson Review*, 11 (Summer 1958), 271–77.

*Brooke-Rose, Christine. "Samuel Beckett and the anti-Novel," *London Magazine*, 5 (Dec. 1958), 38–46.

*Cohn, Ruby. "Preliminary Observations," *Perspective*, 11 (Autumn 1959), 119–31.

*———. "Still Novel," *Yale French Studies*, 24 (Summer 1959), 48–53.

Davie, Donald. "Kinds of Comedy," Spectrum, 2 (Winter 1958), 25–31.

Esslin, Martin. "The Theatre of the Absurd," *Tulane Drama Review*, 4 (May 1960), 3–15.

[Fraser, G. S. ?] "Waiting for Godot," *Times Literary Supplement*, Feb. 10, 1956.

Friedman, Melvin. "The Achievement of Samuel Beckett," *Books Abroad*, 33 (Summer 1959), 278–81.

––––––. "The Novels of Samuel Beckett," *Comparative Literature*, 12 (Winter 1960), 47–58.

––––––. "Samuel Beckett and the Nouveau Roman," *Wisconsin Studies of Contemporary Literature*, 1 (Spring-Summer 1960), 22–36.

Gray, Ronald. "Waiting for Godot: A Christian Interpretation," *Listener*, 57 (Jan. 24, 1957), 160–61.

Gregory, Horace. "Beckett's Dying Gladiators," *Commonweal*, 65 (Oct. 12, 1956), 88–92.

Grossvogel, David. In *The Self-Conscious Stage in Modern French Drama*. New York: Columbia University Press, 1958, pp. 324–34.

*Harvey, Lawrence E. "Art and the Existential in *En Attendant Godot*," *PMLA*, 75 (Mar. 1960), 137–46.

*Hoefer, Jacqueline. "Watt," *Perspective*, 11 (Autumn 1959), 166–82.

*Kenner, Hugh. "The Beckett Landscape," *Spectrum*, 2 (Winter 1958), 8–24.

*––––––. "The Cartesian Centaur," *Perspective*, 11 (Autumn 1959), 132–41. (Probably the most perceptive study of Beckett so far published.)

*Kern, Edith. "Drama Stripped for Inaction: Beckett's *Godot*," *Yale French Studies*, no. 14 (Winter 1954–55), 41–47.

*––––––. "Moran-Molloy: The Hero As Author," *Perspective*, 11 (Autumn 1959), 183–93.

*Loy, J. Robert. "*Things* in Recent French Literature," *PMLA*, 71 (Mar. 1956), 27–41.

Mauriac, Claude. In *The New Literature*. New York: Braziller, 1959, pp. 75–90.

Mayoux, Jean-Jacques. "The Theatre of Samuel Beckett," *Perspective*, 11 (Autumn 1959), 142–55.

Mercier, Vivian. "The Mathematical Limit," *Nation*, 188 (Feb. 14, 1959), 144–45.

*Mintz, Samuel I. "Beckett's *Murphy:* A 'Cartesian' Novel," *Perspective,* 11 (Autumn 1959), 156–65.
*Moore, John R. "A Farewell to Something," *Tulane Drama Review,* 5 (Sept. 1960), 49–60.
*Strauss, Walter A. "Dante's Belacqua and Beckett's Tramps," *Comparative Literature,* 11 (Summer 1959), 250–61.
*Tindall, William Y. "Beckett's Bums," *Critique,* 2 (Spring-Summer 1958), 3–15.

INDEX